Turning the
TIDE

Turning the
TIDE

Real Hope, Real Change.

DR. CHARLES F. STANLEY

HOWARD BOOKS
A DIVISION OF SIMON & SCHUSTER, INC.
New York · Nashville · London · Toronto · Sydney

Howard Books
A Division of Simon & Schuster, Inc.
1230 Avenue of the Americas
New York, NY 10020

Copyright © 2011 by Charles Stanley

All rights reserved, including the right to reproduce this book or portions thereof
in any form whatsoever. For information address Howard Books Subsidiary
Rights Department, 1230 Avenue of the Americas, New York, NY 10020.

First Howard Books hardcover edition June 2011

HOWARD and colophon are trademarks
of Simon & Schuster, Inc.

For information about special discounts for bulk purchases,
please contact Simon & Schuster Special Sales at
1-866-506-1949 or business@simonandschuster.com.

The Simon & Schuster Speakers Bureau can bring authors to your live event.
For more information or to book an event, contact the Simon & Schuster Speakers
Bureau at 1-866-248-3049 or visit our website at www.simonspeakers.com.

Manufactured in the United States of America

10   9   8   7   6   5   4   3   2   1

Library of Congress Control Number: 2011016822

ISBN 978-1-4391-9062-3
ISBN 978-1-4516-1786-3 (ebook)

*Dedicated to the brave men and women
serving in our armed forces.
Thank you for safeguarding America's liberty.*

CONTENTS

PART 1

THE STORY OF
OUR STORM

CHAPTER 1

THE RISING TIDE

The Danger in Failing to Recognize the Storms

Over the years, I have been privileged to see and walk along some of the most magnificent beaches in the world. Not long ago, I was at a Hawaiian seashore known for its tremendous waves—ones worthy of surfing excursions—and I was acutely aware of the rise and fall of the tides.

On several occasions in the past, this particular coastline has had waves that rose more than twenty feet high. A man at the hotel called those times "an extreme surfer's paradise."

While the unfurling and crashing of breakers of that magnitude may excite avid surfers, the rest of us, however, are frightened by such an overpowering crush of water—fantastic to look at, perhaps, but only from a distance.

As I gazed out at the ocean, knowing the potential danger for great waves, my thoughts turned to the painful reality of the tsunami that crashed into Japan in 2011. The devastation in terms of lives and property loss was enormous.

I then began to think about the riptides that can periodically make a beach too dangerous for swimming. Although these tides can be identified by lifeguards and experts as they watch from elevated perches, they are not as easily recognized by beachgoers on the shore or those already in the water. Once an innocent swimmer has been caught in the clutches of such a powerful current, escape is extremely difficult. Rescue is often perilous for those who seek to help. Death is frequently the result.

I considered the rising floodwaters that have devastated many areas in our nation. We live in an age where it is not at all unusual to hear a newscaster report, "Nothing of this magnitude has ever been experienced here before."

I asked myself, *What makes tides go from beautiful to dangerous? What causes the sea to swell and produce a wave that washes away beaches and cities? What creates those waves?*

The answer in many cases is *storms*.

Some of the squalls pound on the surface of the waters, while others occur far away, causing a ripple effect throughout the ocean.

Some tempests involve fierce winds; and others, a seemingly endless amount of heavy rain.

Regardless of how these whirlwinds and downpours occur or where they originate, they cause seismic shifts in the waters—and the tides rise with immensely destructive power.

These observations of nature started me thinking about the issues I will discuss in this book—tempests that occur in our nation and also in our personal lives. These storms don't necessarily have anything to do with weather. They are situations in our lives that devastate us just like a category-five hurricane that ravages a coastal village. They may arise due to our finances, a broken relationship, a lost job, a crippling illness, or any number of distressing circumstances. The dark, threatening clouds roll in—large, turbulent, and overwhelming. They destroy our peace and security, and we cannot escape their fury. We don't know what to do or where to go.

I am convinced that our country is facing just such a storm. We are experiencing a destructive, man-made tide that is deteriorating our country at a frightening pace. And as an American citizen, father, grandfather, and preacher of the Word, I feel the responsibility to speak up about the issues in our country and in our personal lives that require our attention and intercession as believers.

RISING TIDES ON MANY FRONTS

The storms of life cause tides to mount—even to the point of overwhelming us with tragedy, turmoil, and deeply rooted fears.

We experience catastrophic times, not just natural, everyday problems but also man-made disasters. Sadly, if we don't come to grip with our crises and learn how to manage effectively through them, we will continue to find ourselves in increasingly desperate times.

> As an American citizen, father, grandfather, and preacher of the Word, I feel the responsibility to speak up about the issues in our country and in our personal lives that require our attention and intercession as believers.

Just as our personal tempests can devastate our lives if we do not respond to them appropriately, cataclysmic storms can drastically affect our nation as well. So, after my experience on that Hawaiian beach, I sat down to make a list of the storms our country is currently undergoing. I came up with twenty concerns that I truly believe warrant prayer and godly action.

Not all of the items on my list are equal in weight, nor are they presented here in order of priority. However, I believe they are all important in terms of our nation's health and spiritual welfare. If we fail to properly address these storms, they will eventually become an insurmountable tide that will erode our freedoms as citizens of the United States of America.

Below are the issues and conditions I believe are impacting our country negatively:

1. *Mortgage problems:* Many people are unable to pay their mortgages and are losing their homes. This not only affects the

families that become homeless but also impacts their neighborhoods, communities, and all of us as a nation.

2. *Increasing unemployment:* Millions of people have lost their jobs and even more families suffer because they cannot pay their bills or afford their necessities.

3. *Banking issues:* Our nation is facing an overwhelming financial crisis, which includes the insolvency of many banks, tremendous losses for depositors and investors, escalating costs, an excessive national debt, and the weakening of our currency on the international market.

4. *Corrupt leaders:* Our nation is plagued with cowardice, confusion, and corruption in its leadership—on both sides of the aisle. We are in desperate need of godly legislators who will acknowledge the Lord and obey Him.

5. *Ongoing warfare:* As warring continues, the death and wounding of our young men and women escalates. We often send brave soldiers into battle without adequate protective gear, which is absolutely unthinkable.

6. *Terrorism:* The ever-present threat of terrorism erodes our national confidence, endangers our citizens, and jeopardizes our economy.

7. *Natural disasters:* Hurricanes, tornadoes, floods, and other natural disasters are occurring in record-breaking numbers and strengths.

8. *Abortion:* The problem of abortion is ongoing. More than 55 million unborn babies have been killed—and that number is still rising.

9. *Divorce:* The percentage of marriages that end in divorce continues to escalate.

10. *Single-parent families:* Millions of single parents are struggling to raise their children, and the number of kids who are unable to experience a stable home life continues to rise.

11. *Escalating crime:* Our country is experiencing a greater incidence of criminal offenses and lack of justice for victims. Law enforcement officials are frequently unable to protect citizens because of bureaucracy and legal challenges.

12. *America's standing in the world:* Around the world is a rising hatred of Americans that includes the threat of nuclear proliferation by our enemies against our nation and allies.

13. *Diminishing support of Israel:* A desire to appease political rivals has resulted in the deterioration of our national support of Israel.

14. *Challenges to our Judeo-Christian values:* Our freedoms of religion and expression are sometimes denied—especially when it comes to Christians who openly profess Jesus Christ as the only way to the Father.

15. *Fuel availability and pricing:* Even though we are a nation with vast energy resources, the availability of gasoline is not assured and prices are often unpredictable.

16. *Redefining of marriage:* Attempts to redefine marriage undermine our nation's morality.

17. *Illegal immigration:* The problem of illegal immigration not only impacts our economy and safety but also creates an

invisible underclass of many who may genuinely wish to be a vital and productive part of our society.

18. *Toleration of immorality:* An increasing number of religious denominations tolerate immorality as well as accept and support sinful lifestyles even among the clergy.

19. *False prophets:* Because of a lack of biblical literacy in our nation, more and more false prophets have arisen with heretical teachings and counterfeit "gospels."

20. *Need for revival:* One of our country's greatest needs is for true revival and spiritual awakening. Our nation has drifted away from God, and the name of Jesus is openly opposed by many Americans. We must return to a humble, godly reverence of our Sovereign Lord.

It is no wonder that I feel a burden for my nation and an urgency to pray. I have absolutely no doubt that . . .

- The tides are rising.

- Our nation is under serious threat.

- If we don't act decisively and quickly, we will suffer loss and persecution as you and I have never experienced before.

A CALL TO REVERSE THE TRENDS

In ancient times, before there were radars or any of the technological advancements that we're accustomed to today, sailors had almost no warning of incoming storms. Seafarers would set sail on open waters and take their chances in their primitive fishing vessels, with only their skills and faith to protect them. When tempests approached, churning the oceans and tossing about the ships, there was not much the sailors could do. So they would take rope and lash themselves to the mast of the boat. That way, when the wind and the waves hit the hull and thrashed against the deck, they wouldn't be washed overboard.

I believe this is an example of what God wants us to do in the midst of this devastating storm. We are to lash ourselves to the Lord. We are to be in unity and oneness with Him—securely tied to the Father because He can get us safely through this tempest.

> If we fail to properly address these storms, they will eventually become an insurmountable tide that will erode our freedoms as citizens of the United States of America.

Right from the beginning of this book, I want to make it clear that I am calling for serious change in our nation. There are crucial issues we absolutely must address if we hope to preserve the values and principles that have made our land great. Some may believe it is impossible to change the course of our country—that it is too immense a ship to turn around in a storm that is too difficult to survive. I agree; it is. But I also know that "With people it is impossible, but not with God; for all things are possible with God" (Mark 10:27). We *can* change our nation if we turn back to the Lord, lashing ourselves to Him and walking in oneness with Him.

With that said, I would like to state for the record that I am a citizen of the United States of America and I love my country. It is also important to understand that I am not against government—I believe it plays an essential role in any civilized society. For any group to be successful, it must have rules and protocols that guide how it conducts its business. This is true whether the organization is a corporation, a church, or a nation.

Likewise, I am not trying to convince any American to become part of either a political party or the Christian denomination to which I belong. Rather, my approach has been to speak with people from all walks of life, to meet with leaders, and to do everything I can to support and defend the foundational values and principles that form the indispensible framework of our Constitution. As a Christian in the United States, I have the right—as well as the duty—to speak openly about matters of government, leadership, and societal trends.

Through this book, I hope to encourage every citizen to stand up for the freedoms he or she enjoys as an American and to ensure that this liberty continues for future generations. I especially make a personal appeal to you as a Christian. I firmly believe that it is not only the privilege but the responsibility of every believer to become actively involved in the preservation of godly principles in whatever nation he or she calls home.

I hope to encourage every citizen to stand up for the freedoms he or she enjoys as an American and to ensure that this liberty continues for future generations.

Therefore, consider this book a clarion call for *you* to speak up, stand up, and pray as never before. If you desire the ungodly trends in our nation to be reversed, understand that it will happen only if you and I and others who believe as we do fight this battle on our knees before the Father and obey Him wholeheartedly. We must lash ourselves to the Lord and walk in oneness with Him.

A CALL TO PURSUE GOD'S HIGHEST AND BEST

As a Christian, you have the unique challenge of simultaneously living in two worlds. You live in this natural world, where you have responsibilities to your community and nation. You are also a citizen of the kingdom of God and are accountable to the Lord Almighty (see Philippians 3:20–21).

Jesus readily acknowledged this duality in our lives
(see Matthew 22:15–22), but He also made these two things very
clear:

1. Our primary allegiance and responsibility is always to the
Father.

2. Our existence should impact the earth—including our
government—by the way we live out our heavenly values.
Jesus said we are to be like salt and light to this world
(see Matthew 5:13–16). We are to preserve all that is good and
be obedient, godly agents of change for the Lord's glory and so
others may be saved.

In the vast majority of cases, we will most likely find that the choices
we make concerning the current national atmosphere and the everlasting kingdom of God are not merely a matter of "one or the other."
We are not called to disengage from
our communities to serve the Father or
vice versa. Rather, God calls us to look
beyond "good" to "best"—to pursue
the very highest principles and goals,

> God's desire is for us to experi-
> ence life at its very best—both in
> this world and the one to come.

whether we are here on earth influencing our leaders or enjoying eternity in heaven with Him. His desire is for us to experience life at its
very best—both in this world and the one to come.

A CALL TO ACT *NOW*

In view of the storm that is assailing our nation and the rising tide
that threatens to destroy the land we know and love, we have no time
to spare, waste, or hesitate. The time for action is now.

Scriptural Warnings

Throughout Scripture, we find warnings from God—given to us because He cares for and loves us. He told Israel in Deuteronomy 32:46–47, "Take to your heart all the words with which I am warning you today, which you shall command your sons to observe carefully, even all the words of this law. For it is not an idle word for you; indeed it is your life. And by this word you will prolong your days."

His admonitions are for our good, not to hurt us or impede our progress. On the contrary, the Lord wants to protect us from harm and place us in the best possible position to receive His tremendous blessings and rewards. Therefore, the Father's warnings for us should be heard and obeyed with a sense of urgency.

Likewise, we must never assume that God's cautions and rebukes are for somebody else or merely for a people who live in another time and place. Such an assumption is always a great mistake. The Bible is clear that those who fail to heed the Lord's discipline—whether nations, cities, or individuals—suffer devastating consequences. Rather, we must examine our hearts and make sure they are clean—confessing and repenting of our sins whenever He reveals their presence to us.

The core of what we wrestle with is, of course, the free will that God has given to all human beings. This gift allows us to make choices about whether we will obey or disobey the Father. We have the ability to decide whether we will accept the Savior's invitation of mercy, forgiveness, and relationship—or refuse it. We can consciously choose whether to have faith in God and follow the daily directives He gives us through the Holy Spirit or to reject Him—trusting in ourselves and following our own impulses and desires.

This means that for us to truly heed the Lord's warnings, we must make a conscious choice to align our will with His.

The Consequences of Disobedience

We see this truth from the opening pages of the Bible. Adam and Eve lived in paradise. All the Garden of Eden was theirs to enjoy, with only one caveat: "From any tree of the garden you may eat freely; but from the tree of the knowledge of good and evil you shall not eat, for in the day that you eat from it you will surely die" (Genesis 2:16–17).

You would think they would have been wise enough to say, "We have everything we could ever want—why risk it all for one bite of fruit?" Nevertheless, the couple refused to heed God's warning and took the destructive path of disobedience. They ate of the tree and suffered the consequences, and the course of history was changed in an instant.

Throughout the centuries, we see the same mistake repeated: individuals, cities, and nations hear the truth; ignore it; choose their own way rather than God's; and endure the terrible outcome of their short-sighted defiance. This is why Hebrews 12:25 cautions, "See to it that you do not refuse Him who is speaking. For if those did not escape when they refused him who warned them on earth, much less will we escape who turn away from Him who warns from heaven."

We are in a similar situation today spiritually as a nation. We willfully drift away from the Father's life-giving commands and refuse to heed His rebuke. And unless this tide of disobedience is reversed, we too—like many civilizations before us—will suffer disastrous consequences. This is not speculation—it is the truth as evidenced throughout history. What the Lord says *will* come to pass.

What the Lord says *will* come to pass.

HOW *YOU* CAN HELP TURN THE TIDE

At the end of each chapter, you will find a few questions based on the concepts shared in this book. The focus of these questions is on what *you* can do as a Christian and as a citizen of the United States to make a difference in our country. I challenge you to pray about these questions and answer them in the manner that the Father directs you. It is my prayer that these questions will help you discover who God wants you to become so you can carry out the mission He has for you.

―――――――

Open our eyes, Lord, to see our nation
as You see it. Give us sorrow for those
things that sadden Your heart.
Give us the resolve to confess and repent of our sinful
ways that we might draw closer to You
and experience more of Your presence,
provision, and protection.

―――――――

HOW *YOU* CAN HELP TURN THE TIDE

1. *"We are to lash ourselves to the Lord. We are to be in unity and oneness with Him—securely tied to the Father because He can get us safely through this tempest."*

The above statement by Dr. Stanley is one of the core principles that will help us weather our country's storms, having made important contributions to our nation's well-being. What does it mean for you, personally, to lash yourself to the Lord? What would it mean for our country? Think about it this way: when you're "lashed" to something or someone, you are forced to abandon your own efforts and rely solely on the one you are lashed to. What do you—and our nation—need to abandon in order to be lashed to the Lord?

2. Dr. Stanley says that the ungodly trends in our nation will be reversed only *"if you and I and others who believe as we do fight this battle on our knees before the Father and obey Him wholeheartedly."*

Will you commit to fighting this battle on your knees before the Father and obeying Him wholeheartedly? Think about what this means on a practical level: What part of your day can you set aside for prayer? What in your life do you need to change in order to obey God without reservation or hesitation? Only by beginning with personal transformation can we help to turn the tide of our nation.

3. Dr. Stanley reminds us that *"our primary allegiance and responsibility is always to the Father. Our existence should impact*

the earth—including our government—by the way we live out our heavenly values."

How can you, personally, impact the earth and our government by the way you live out your heavenly values? Be as specific as you can.

4. In this chapter, Dr. Stanley says: *"We must never assume that God's cautions and rebukes are for somebody else. . . . We must examine our hearts and make sure they are clean—confessing and repenting of our sins whenever He reveals their presence to us."*

What cautions from God have you pointed toward others before examining your own heart? Will you spend some time in prayer with God, asking Him to reveal the sins that you need to confess and repent of? The more pure our own hearts become, the more useful we will be in helping our nation become what it needs to be.

CHAPTER 2

REAL HOPE

*We Must Trade In Shallow Optimism
for Genuine Hope and Change*

A fter any major election, there is always an abundance of post-vote analysis. Newsmakers will explore topics such as: What did the triumphant candidates and their operatives do right in order to gain the victory? What did the losing side do wrong? What outside sources affected the outcome of the contest?

Generally, commentators will cite a wide spectrum of explanations for the results—from the weather to issues about states' rights. And all sorts of people and groups come forward to take credit for the win.

GOD'S INVOLVEMENT
IN OUR NATION

However, it is interesting to note that I rarely hear anyone in the media report that the Lord had anything to do with an election. They attribute the candidate's success to any number of superficial reasons—the person was taller or his name was first alphabetically—and they refuse to admit that any spiritual explanation could possibly be the cause. Why?

The truth of the matter is that, sadly, many people believe that *if* God exists—and many do not think He does—He is just a spectator on the sidelines, watching to see what Americans will do, with no real role in the life of our country.

As believers, we know the truth: the Lord is never a mere bystander in any situation. Daniel 2:20–21 explains, "Let the name of God be blessed forever and ever, For wisdom and power belong to Him. It is He who changes the times and the epochs; He removes kings and establishes kings." In one way or another, He is involved in every circumstance of our lives. This is especially true when nations as a whole are involved. Voters in a representative republic may elect a few individuals to be stewards of the government, but ultimately, we must acknowledge that God is the One in control. Only He can truly help our country. He is our only true hope.

> God is the One in control. Only He can truly help our country.

CAN ANY *PERSON* TRULY TURN US AROUND?

In the aftermath of the 1980 presidential election that resulted in what many called a "landslide" victory for Ronald Reagan, a major news magazine asked: "Reagan: Can He Turn Us Around?"

The answer was *yes*, to some extent. But it was also partly *no*.

It would have been unfair for the millions who voted for Reagan—or any person, for that matter—to think his election meant that all of the nation's problems would be solved the moment he took office or in the eight years he served. He had to address profound energy issues, continuing conflicts in the Middle East, the threat of the Union of Soviet Socialist Republics' (USSR) ongoing military buildup, economic instability, increasing immorality, and an unprecedented rise in crime. The challenge was, in most respects, absolutely insurmountable—even for the most talented leader or legislative body.

But the truth of the matter is that it is imprudent to think that *anyone* can singlehandedly change a nation or resolve all of its problems. Yes, history shows that Reagan indeed had great success as president, and he improved the lives of many Americans. His election ushered in a new spirit of optimism, which seemed to sweep across the nation. Many throughout the land began to genuinely believe that the country could recover and that their lives would get better.

> It is imprudent to think that *anyone* can singlehandedly change a nation or resolve all of its problems.

In fact, the Misery Index—an economic indicator that is calculated by adding the unemployment rate to the rise of inflation—dropped from nearly 22 percent to an average of 12 percent during Reagan's two terms. People were again able to find jobs and affordable loans for necessities such as automobiles and houses. People regained a sense of optimism.

It should be noted, however, that *optimism* is not the same as genuine *hope*—at least not in the biblical sense.

Although President Reagan had many excellent accomplishments, the United States continued to wrestle with the same issues that plagued the nation when he took office—the same issues we wrestle with even to this day. He could not permanently change the nation in his own strength or through political channels—and neither can any other person. Placing our hope for a new nation in this one man would have been hope misplaced.

MISPLACED HOPE

We can see the consequences of misplaced hope clearly demonstrated in the history of Israel. For thousands of years, the Jewish people watched for the coming of the Messiah. What they expected was a mighty military and political leader like King David who would forever do away with the stranglehold of foreign rulers. The Messiah they were looking for would inaugurate peace in the land that had been promised to them as their inheritance. He was also supposed to usher in a prosperous kingdom of innumerable blessings.

As believers, we understand that the true Messiah, Jesus of Nazareth, did not come to establish a military or political empire—at least, not yet (see Revelation 1:5–8; 19:11–21). He first came as the Suffering Servant to establish the spiritual kingdom of God and provide salvation to whomever would believe in Him (see Isaiah 53).

But because so many in Israel were so intensely focused on earthly success and security—rather than on the Father's plan—they missed the One they were truly yearning for. Their hope was placed in the wrong thing.

This sad reality caused Jesus to lament, "Jerusalem, Jerusalem, who kills the prophets and stones those who are sent to her! How often I wanted to gather your children together, the way a hen gathers her chicks under her wings, and you were unwilling. Behold, your house is being left to you desolate!" (Matthew 23:37–38).

The point is this: any time we look to a president or official to do what only God can do, we are asking for trouble. Our eyes are on the wrong person and a mistaken goal. Furthermore, any time a leader calls upon us to do for ourselves what only the Savior can do in us, we are likewise being misled.

> Any time we look to a president or official to do what only God can do, we are asking for trouble.

How wise the psalmist who wrote, "Do not trust in princes, In mortal man, in whom there is no salvation. His spirit departs, he returns to the earth; In that very day his thoughts perish" (Psalm 146:3–4).

THE NATURE OF REAL HOPE

Part of our problem is that *hope* is often defined as a wish for something good to happen or for a longing to come true. We "hope" our team will win, our 401(k) will increase in value, or a runaway child will find his way home. It is an emotion rooted in the desire for life to be better.

There is nothing wrong with being positive or eager for beneficial news. As I mentioned earlier, however, the optimism that the world inspires in us can never be considered true hope—not as it is described in the Bible. Hope founded upon a human being, a man-made philosophy, or any institution is always misplaced. Why? Because these things are unreliable and fleeting. They do not last (see James 1:10–11; 1 John 2:17).

Rather, to be genuine and enduring, our confidence and hope must be rooted in God and His eternal purposes.

You see, the Lord desires for us to base our faith on what is sure, immovable, unchangeable, and unending. As our Savior, Jesus gives us the one thing that can never be taken away— everlasting life (see John 10:27–30).

> To be genuine and enduring, our confidence and hope must be rooted in God and His eternal purposes.

He has forgiven our sins so we can be reconciled to the Father and enjoy a home with Him in heaven forever. We read in 1 Peter 1:3–5,

> *Blessed be the God and Father of our Lord Jesus Christ, who according to His great mercy has caused us to be born again to a* living hope *through the resurrection of Jesus Christ from the dead,* to obtain *an inheritance which is imperishable and undefiled and will not fade away, reserved in heaven for you, who are protected by the power of God through faith for a salvation ready to be revealed in the last time. (Roman type used for emphasis.)*

Imperishable. Undefiled. Unfading. This is true hope—the unshakable confidence and assurance Jesus offers us. The writer to the Hebrews affirms, "This hope we have as an anchor of the soul, a hope both sure and steadfast" (Hebrews 6:19).

GODLY HOPE COMPELS CHANGE

Authentic hope, which is rooted and established in God, is powerful. It effectively transforms the life of the individual who embraces it. In fact, because of the eternal nature of our confidence, a person who lives by faith in Christ should conduct his or her life in a vastly different manner than one who is still dependent on earthly sources of security. The apostle John taught us this when he wrote the following:

> *Beloved, now we are children of God, and it has not appeared as yet what we will be. We know that when He appears, we will be like Him, because we will see Him just as He is. And everyone who has this hope fixed on Him purifies himself, just as He is pure. (1 John 3:2–3)*

As people who have this genuine hope, we should choose to live in a distinctive way—abstaining from sin and practicing righteousness because of our inherent desire to honor the Lord (see 1 John 3:7). This means setting our hearts and minds on Jesus and living out the life of Christ in our unique circumstances.

> **We should choose to live in a distinctive way—abstaining from sin and practicing righteousness because of our inherent desire to honor the Lord.**

When we do so, we find that hope is inextricably tied to faith and love (see 1 Corinthians 13:13). In order to survive life's trials and tidal waves, our expectations must be rooted in absolute trust of the Savior's matchless character (see Hebrews 11:1, 6). Likewise, our confidence in Him must have a godly outlet—we must live out our hope through loving obedience to Him and the compassionate care we show to others (see John 13:34–35).

What we discover is that the constant renewal of our faith in Jesus and the consistent expression of our love for Him and others results in the fortification of our hope—and vice versa. Repeatedly, the truth that there is nowhere safer than in the center of God's will is reinforced in us; and our faith, hope, and love become more firmly fixed in our hearts.

Our intimate relationship with the Father grows, as does our confidence that He is in control of the present and of our eternal future and that He always provides us with His very best. We become absolutely certain that He can be trusted to do what He says He will do—which is the very definition of the hope we're pursuing.

THE HIGHER PURPOSE OF GODLY HOPE

As we mature in our faith, hope, and love, our perspective changes as well. Because our confidence and expectations are based on the everlasting life we receive through faith in Jesus, it should be no surprise that our love for other eternal things also increases. That is, our longing to spend time in the Word of God and in fellowship with other spirit-filled believers will grow. We become compelled to share the gospel with others because we want them to experience the same assurance and anticipation that we do (see 2 Corinthians 5:14–15).

Mere optimism cannot motivate us in the awesome, life-changing, eternal way that godly hope can. This is because the goal of an optimistic outlook is limited—we simply wish to achieve our desires. However, true, biblical

> True, biblical hope recognizes that only Jesus is worthy of being our standard—He is our goal. So we strive to become like Him in every way possible.

hope recognizes that only Jesus is worthy of being our standard—He is our goal. So we strive to become like Him in every way possible (see Romans 8:29). In faith, we seek to deepen our intimate relationship with Him and align our lives with the principles in Scripture so we will honor Him in all we say and do.

In this way, we do not merely take hold of temporary earthly objectives, though we may enjoy attaining them in the process. Instead, we take hold of what the Father wants for us, for what He achieves in us is everlasting: we become people of godly character who reflect His glory and do works that further His eternal purposes.

WHAT ARE BELIEVERS TO DO?

In light of the differences between optimism and true biblical hope, how can Christians ensure we remain on a path that honors the Lord and His eternal purposes—regardless of the earthly issues that arise during elections?

1. Intentionally Pursue the Genuine Hope Christ Offers

Whether we are pleased or disappointed by the results of an election, we must remember that God is in control. Our hope is in Him, not in our candidate of choice. We should become neither arrogant if our candidate wins nor discouraged if he loses. Our objectives must remain the same:

1. To seek an intimate relationship with the Father.

2. To obey God and leave all the consequences to Him.

In this way, we stay on track—nourishing the hope we have in Christ and experiencing the true inner revival that can come only by daily communion with Him.

2. Recognize That God Is Still at Work

Remember, it is the Lord who "puts down one and exalts another" (Psalm 75:7). Romans 13:1 confirms: "Every person is to be in subjection to the governing authorities. For there is no authority except from God, and those which exist are established by God." The future of our nation remains safe in His capable hands. We may not always understand His reasons for allowing certain individuals to hold office, but we can be confident in His eternal purposes, nonetheless.

The Father's desire is that believers continue to trust, obey, and hope in Him, regardless of who is in power. We must be open to His leading and submit to His plan. This means:

1. We should be diligent in praying for our leaders.

2. We should seek the Father through prayer and time in His Word, and we should encourage those in office to do so as well.

3. We should provide an example of responsible citizenship to those around us.

4. We should be respectful in the way we talk and think about our leaders.

5. And we should respond out of love and compassion whenever we're given an opportunity to minister to those who are hurting—such as widows, orphans, and those who have lost their homes and their jobs.

3. Understand the True Reason for the Issues Assailing Our Country

Our national troubles are never solely economic, diplomatic, ideological, or technological—there are always deeper spiritual issues at work. We must ask the Father to give us wisdom about them and do our best to honor Him in them.

> **Our national troubles are never solely economic, diplomatic, ideological, or technological—there are always deeper spiritual issues at work.**

For example, if God's goal is to discipline the country so we will turn back to Him spiritually, we should examine our hearts and repent of our sinfulness—encouraging others to do the same.

If the Father is teaching us about the futility of our earthly wealth and security so the lost will learn to rely upon Him for salvation, we should be available for Him to use as ministers of His grace.

If the Lord blesses us with prosperity, it may be so we will have the resources we need to proclaim the gospel to all nations.

We must ask God to help us understand the profound problems we face and obey whatever He calls us to do in order to correct them.

4. Remember That in the Father's Eyes, People Aren't Our Enemies—Sin Is

Never lose sight of the fact that each person—regardless of his or her political leanings—is in need of a personal relationship with Jesus Christ. Yes, it is important that we take a stand on the significant matters that are being legislated. However, we should never do so in a manner that would disgrace the name of Jesus or hinder others from accepting Him as their Savior.

Nothing is more important than a person's soul. So remember to show love and grace to others—even if you don't agree with them (see 2 Timothy 2:14). The goal is always to lead them to the genuine, eternal hope that can be found only in Jesus.

WE ARE ALL RESPONSIBLE

Now, there may be people who question whether Christians should be involved in issues of government at all—especially considering that the concept of the representative republic is relatively recent. However, I do not find one verse in Scripture that calls us to disengage from the responsibilities of citizenship.

On the contrary, Proverbs 11:11 (TLB) teaches us, "The good influence of godly citizens causes a city to prosper."

Also, the apostle Paul instructed, "I urge that entreaties and prayers, petitions and thanksgivings, be made on behalf of all men, for kings and all who are in authority, so that we may lead a tranquil and quiet life in all godliness and dignity. This is good and acceptable in the sight of God our Savior" (1 Timothy 2:1–3).

The Bible speaks at great length about how godly men such as Nathan, Elijah, Daniel, and Nehemiah influenced kings for the good of their people. What this tells me is that we need to be actively involved in overcoming the issues that confront us as a nation—whether we are fighting the battle on our knees or writing to our lawmakers to influence their votes. This tells me that our hope in God compels us to proactively influence those who are in power.

Remember, our government was established for our protection—that is its main role. The responsibility of our elected officials is to safeguard us from both foreign and domestic enemies who seek to harm or destroy us. And our duty as citizens is to hold them accountable.

> We need to be actively involved in overcoming the issues that confront us as a nation.

ANOTHER EXAMPLE FROM HISTORY

As I mentioned earlier, the prophet Daniel did a great deal to shape the opinions of the ruling authorities for the sake of the Jewish people. In fact, Daniel's influence spanned almost seventy years—during both the Babylonian and Medo-Persian empires and through the reigns of multiple kings. His influence was powerful because he knew where to place his hope. He trusted in God above all else.

Daniel was just a teenager when he was taken to Babylon in 605 BC, during what would be the first of three deportations from the nation of Judah. He was chosen for the king's service, where he distinguished himself almost immediately—becoming known for his knowledge, intelligence, and abilities.

One night, the Babylonian king, Nebuchadnezzar, had a terribly disturbing dream. He awoke feeling profoundly anxious and troubled. Without delay, Nebuchadnezzar sent for the magicians and wise men of his court and demanded that they tell him what he had dreamed and what his dream meant. He then added, "If you do not make known to me the dream and its interpretation, you will be torn limb from limb and your houses will be made a rubbish heap" (Daniel 2:5).

The sorcerers and counselors were dumbfounded. They had no answer for him—how could they? When they told the king that his command was impossible to carry out, Nebuchadnezzar ordered that all the wise men of Babylon be executed, including Daniel.

Daniel heard of the death sentence and asked the king for time to consult God on the matter. That evening, he joined in prayer with three other Hebrew exiles in the king's service—Hananiah, Mishael, and Azariah. During the night, the Lord revealed to Daniel the vision and its interpretation. The young prophet awoke with this word of praise on his lips:

> *"Let the name of God be blessed forever and ever,*
> *For wisdom and power belong to Him.*
> *It is He who changes the times and the epochs;*
> *He removes kings and establishes kings;*
> *He gives wisdom to wise men*

And knowledge to men of understanding.
It is He who reveals the profound and hidden things;
He knows what is in the darkness,
And the light dwells with Him.
To You, O God of my fathers, I give thanks and praise,
For You have given me wisdom and power;
Even now You have made known to me what we requested
   of You,
For You have made known to us the king's matter."
   (Daniel 2:20–23)

When Daniel went before Nebuchadnezzar, he was able to tell the king all he wanted to know about the dream and what it meant. More important, however, is that Daniel revealed to Whom Nebuchadnezzar was ultimately accountable—the Lord God Almighty. The young prophet rightly attributed all of the glory to the Father when he said, "There is a God in heaven who reveals mysteries, and He has made known to King Nebuchadnezzar what will take place" (Daniel 2:28).

At this point, it is important to notice three things:

1. No King or Leader Knows Everything by Means of His Own Study or Personal Experience

No government official can possibly have all the answers necessary to solve all the problems a nation faces. Although Babylon was a very advanced empire at the time, Nebuchadnezzar realized that he had absolutely no idea what his dream meant or what he was supposed to do about it. The same is often true for today's leaders. They deal with so many diverse issues that they could not possibly be experts on all of them. They must rely on the counsel of their advisors to make their decisions—which is not always optimal.

2. God Knows

Thankfully, the Lord has profound wisdom about all things. He sees from the beginning to the end of every matter, and understands the absolute best course to take in every situation. When we place our hope and confidence in Him, we will not fail.

3. The Father Will Reveal What We Need to Know When We Ask Him for His Wisdom

The great promise of James 1:5 is this: "If any of you lacks wisdom, let him ask of God, who gives to all generously and without reproach, and it will be given to him." There is only one requirement: we must "ask in faith," which means we cannot doubt the Lord's response (James 1:6).

> The Lord sees from the beginning to the end of every matter and understands the absolute best course to take in every situation.

When Daniel received God's answer, he understood and trusted that he had been given exactly what he needed and immediately praised the Father for His provision. The prophet did not hesitate or question the revelation; rather, he acknowledged the Lord's goodness and sovereignty.

WHAT WE SHOULD DO AND WHAT WE CAN EXPECT

So how can you and I influence our leaders as Daniel did? There are four aspects of his story that are worth a closer look. These four teachings show us what we should do—and the response we can expect—when we approach God for His wisdom and provision.

1. No Preconceptions—Simply Go Before Him with a Humble Heart

The first thing we should note is that Daniel asked Hananiah, Mishael, and Azariah to join him in prayer, without first forming opinions or assumptions about Nebuchadnezzar's dream. The four young men went humbly before the Father to seek His guidance and "request compassion from the God of heaven concerning this mystery, so that Daniel and his friends would not be destroyed" (Daniel 2:18). We would be wise to do the same.

2. Wait Patiently for the Lord's Answer

Second, after Daniel prayed, he waited for God to respond. Keep in mind that those four Hebrew youths were facing a death sentence. Yet the prophet went to sleep, confident in the Father's provision and wisdom. What an example of complete trust and hope in the Lord!

Many people are so busy in the pursuit of their desires that they fail to pause long enough to hear the Lord. They fear that if they take time to wait before God, they will miss out on vital opportunities. However, nothing could be further from the truth. There is absolutely nothing more important we can do with our time than wait on God in prayer.

I believe it is crucial that we sit still and pay attention to what the Father is saying to us. After all, listening to God is absolutely essential if we hope to walk with Him.

3. Acknowledge That He Has Given You Complete Information

Third, we should realize that the Lord revealed all Daniel needed to know about the king's dream, including the meaning of each detail. Daniel didn't wait to hear more from the Father. Rather, the prophet trusted that he had been given all he needed to proceed.

The same is true for us. Whenever the Lord gives us a command, we should do as He says immediately. We can trust that He will take full responsibility for our needs as we obey Him—including providing us with all pertinent information.

> God's plans and purposes may unfold over time, but we can be confident that He will always give us everything we require to succeed.

God's plans and purposes may unfold over time, but we can be confident that He will always give us everything we require to succeed. Our responsibility is to keep listening, trusting, and obeying.

4. Respond to Him in Praise

Finally, we should see that Daniel's immediate reaction to the Lord's provision was to praise God as the only One who can reveal such mysteries (see Daniel 2:27–28). The prophet did not see this triumph as an opportunity to glean favor for himself. Rather, he rightly recognized it as God's victory and consistently attributed all of the glory to the Father.

Daniel bravely acknowledged that it was the Lord God Almighty who had supplied the answers that Nebuchadnezzar needed (see Daniel 2:45). In response, the king proclaimed, "Surely your God is a God of gods and a Lord of kings and a revealer of mysteries, since you have been able to reveal this mystery" (Daniel 2:47). And because of Daniel's courageous testimony, King Nebuchadnezzar began the journey that would eventually lead him to "praise, exalt and honor the King of heaven" (Daniel 4:37).

WHAT ABOUT YOU?

Of course, you may be wondering, *Can I truly hear the Father's voice and receive answers to my questions? Can I really be like Daniel and influence those in office with God's own wisdom?* You absolutely can! In Jeremiah 33:3 the Lord promises, "Call to Me and I will answer you, and I will tell you great and mighty things, which you do not know." This is a promise that elicits true hope.

Likewise, Jesus taught the disciples, "When they bring you before the synagogues and the rulers and the authorities, do not worry about how or what you are to speak in your defense, or what you are to say; for the Holy Spirit will teach you in that very hour what you ought to say" (Luke 12:11–12).

And He did! When the disciples faced questioning by the Jewish rulers, Acts 4:13 records, "As they [the elders and scribes]

They had been with Jesus.

---

observed the confidence of Peter and John and understood that they were uneducated and untrained men, they were amazed, and began to recognize them as *having been with Jesus*." (Italics added for emphasis.)

If uneducated fishermen left such an impression on the scholarly temple officials, how much more can you—with all of your gifts, training, and experience—influence the leaders of our nation? But you must notice the key: *they had been with Jesus*. As I often say, your intimacy with God determines the impact that your life has on others.

THE BIBLICAL CALL FOR SERVANT LEADERSHIP

As you spend time with the Lord, He teaches you His ways and enables you to make decisions that are consistent with His character and holiness. He also demonstrates the secret of truly great leadership: *service.*

Remember, Jesus was very clear: "The Son of Man did not come to be served, but to serve, and to give His life a ransom for many" (Matthew 20:28).

This is what we are called to as believers—to influence our communities and country by actively helping others and showing them God's love and the reason for our hope in Him. The apostle Paul expounded on how we are to act and why it is important. He wrote:

Do nothing from selfishness or empty conceit, but with humility of mind regard one another as more important than yourselves; do not merely look out for your own personal interests, but also for the interests of others. Have this attitude in yourselves which was also in Christ Jesus, who, although He existed in the form of God, did not regard equality with God a thing to be grasped, but emptied Himself, taking the form of a bond-servant. . . . For it is God who is at work in you, both to will and to work for His good pleasure. Do all things without grumbling or disputing; so that you will prove yourselves to be blameless and innocent, children of God above reproach in the midst of a crooked and perverse generation, among whom you appear as lights in the world. (Philippians 2:3–7, 13–15)

This is what we are called to as believers—to influence our communities and country by actively helping others and showing them God's love.

If you recall, earlier in the chapter we discussed real hope and how it inspires faith and love in us. All three—faith, hope, and love—are absolutely foundational to everything the servant leader is and does. Because of our desire to honor the Lord and lead the lost to Him, we must remain humble and compassionate in our dealings with others—even if we disagree with them.

THE SERVANT LEADER'S PATH TO HIGHER GROUND

Servant leadership is a foreign concept to many in political circles. Repeatedly, we hear calls for our government officials to work together. Sadly, time and again, one election after another, there are no solutions to our troubles—only more fighting. At times it seems that our representatives are more interested in having issues to campaign about than finding real answers.

One of the problems, it seems, is that our leaders claim to seek "common ground," but they do so in a manner that does not necessarily inspire teamwork. When people become entrenched in their opinions—often because of years and countless hours of debating their particular positions—they become hardened and unable to come to a cohesive, cooperative settlement with people from across the aisle.

Another difficulty is that often when our lawmakers are finally able to come to a compromise, their solutions make our situation worse, rather than better.

I would suggest, therefore, that instead of "*common* ground," our leaders need to seek "*higher* ground."

There is always the possibility of a third position in any two-person argument or discussion. There are . . .

> **Instead of "*common* ground," our leaders need to seek "*higher* ground."**

your opinion.
my opinion.
God's opinion.

Of course, none of us should ever assume that our view is the same as the Father's. Refusing to place our hope and trust in people rather than God includes our not placing hope in ourselves. We must always seek the Lord's guidance with an open and teachable mind, submitting ourselves to His will in our study of Scripture and in prayer.

When you and another person are unable to find a point of agreement, it is crucial to recognize that God may have a solution in mind that both of you have yet to imagine. Recall the words of the Lord through the prophet Isaiah: "'My thoughts are not your thoughts, nor are your ways My ways,' declares the LORD. 'For as the heavens are higher than the earth, so are My ways higher than your ways and My thoughts than your thoughts'" (Isaiah 55:8–9).

Therefore, when you find yourself in a disagreement with another person—whether in regards to your civic life, work, community, church, or personal relationships—it is very helpful to practice these four steps:

1. Together, Make a Decision That You Will Reach an Agreement

In other words—agree to find something that works for both of you.

2. Set Ground Rules

There may be certain aspects of your position that absolutely *cannot* be modified or altered for any reason because of limitations such as budgetary restrictions or legal responsibilities. Begin with a clear understanding of what the two of you truly cannot change, because this will help to clarify your choices later.

3. Explore Every Option Possible

Once you know what your limitations are, you can begin to consider alternatives to the things that *can* change. As stated earlier, recognize that there may be a plan that neither of you has yet envisioned or fully explored.

If there are points of your disagreement that you do not fully understand, it is helpful for both parties to together seek the expertise of others. Enlist different points of view and, above all, solicit input from people of godly character focused on the issue.

Continue to ask questions in order to find points of agreement:

- What if . . . ?

- What about . . . ?

- Could we . . . ?

- Is it possible that . . . ?

This is not merely brainstorming—though that is part of what you will be doing. Rather, it is coming to a mutual recognition that there are many solutions to most problems, and often, the best solution is within your grasp.

4. Pray Together, Asking God to Reveal His Sovereign Plan

Ask the Father to give you practical ways to continue working together and a mutual understanding of His plan. After all, the Lord knows the answers and solutions we desperately need.

Imagine what awesome things the Father could do in our nation if those in our government would humble themselves, place their hope fully on Him, and call for prayer. It is absolutely amazing what they could accomplish!

Not only would our country finally experience real and lasting change, but people throughout the land would witness the transformational power of genuine hope in the Lord Jesus Christ.

And that, my friend, would certainly be worth reporting.

Help us, Lord. Open our eyes so that we may
recognize our sinfulness and repent. Show us how to rely solely
on the eternal hope that You give us,
rather than the empty optimism of this world.
Draw the leaders of this nation to Yourself in renewed
humility and faith. May those who do not know You
accept Jesus as their Lord and Savior.
Help us to wait patiently before You
until we know Your answer, and please fill us with
the courage to pursue Your will
with all our heart, mind, soul, and strength. Amen.

HOW *YOU* CAN HELP TURN THE TIDE

1. In this chapter, Dr. Stanley reminds us that *"Optimism is not the same as genuine hope—at least not in the biblical sense."*

What did you learn in this chapter about the difference between optimism and hope? Whom or what is your hope in? You'll find some answers to that question as you review how you spend your time and money. Do some honest soul-searching and prepare your heart to better serve our country.

2. *"Yes, it is important that we take a stand on the significant matters that are being legislated. However, we should never do so in a manner that would disgrace the name of Jesus or hinder others from accepting Him as their Savior."*

What specific actions might Dr. Stanley be talking about in the statement above? How can we effectively take important stands, yet do so in a way that won't disgrace the name of Jesus or hinder others from coming to Him?

3. *"Your intimacy with God determines the impact that your life has on others."*

Reread Acts 4:12. As Dr. Stanley points out, the strength of Peter and John's influence on the religious leaders of their time was in direct proportion to the fact that they had "been with Jesus." Examine your own life to make sure you are spending time with Jesus and His Word before you begin your efforts to affect our leaders.

CHAPTER 3

WHERE WE HAVE FAILED

The Way into This Mess Reveals the Way out of It

If a person is going to succeed, there are two things that he or she must prayerfully and conscientiously consider:

- Where has he been?

- Where is she going?

Why?

First, a person who doesn't have a clear understanding of his or her history is prone to repeat past mistakes. And, as we're often told, doing the same thing over and over, while expecting different results, is one of the definitions of insanity.

Second, it's important for an individual to comprehend what he or she desires to achieve, because a person who doesn't have intelligible objectives is just wandering through life. It is only when you have an aspiration that is both powerfully moving and inspiring that you become focused in your use of time, energy, and talents.

Of course, this is true for individuals as well as governments and political systems.

I have enjoyed reading and studying history all my life. I believe that investigating the successes and failures of past empires and civilizations can be instructive, motivational, and a great defense against avoidable mistakes. This is especially true when we examine the results of nations as they have either honored God's Word or intentionally challenged His purposes.

This kind of pursuit sensitizes us to the critical moments in our country that have altered our course away from success and toward failure. We realize which factors are causing the difficulties we are currently experiencing and are therefore equipped to reverse the destructive trends.

> **Studying the past helps us know what we wish to become; it clarifies where we have been and where we have gone astray.**

In other words, studying the past helps us know what we wish to become; it clarifies where we have been and where we have gone astray.

HALLMARKS OF A GODLY NATION

In examining history and meditating upon Scripture, I have come to the conclusion that godly nations exhibit five powerful and motivational characteristics:

1. Laws that are consistent with the Word of God.

2. Leaders who acknowledge that they are ultimately accountable to the Lord.

3. The recognizable presence of a growing, vibrant, Christ-centered body of believers that influences its society in a powerful way through its love for the Father and compassion for fellow citizens.

4. A prevailing spirit of awe and humility before the Lord among all the people of the land.

5. The willingness of the people and leaders to call upon and honor the Lord, both in times of crisis and in seasons of prosperity.

These are the principles that produce success in a country—and we should pursue them if we wish for the United States to endure. Sadly, as seen in the failures revealed below, there is overwhelming evidence that our nation is drifting further away from these foundational tenets than ever before.

FAILURE #1: A DEPARTURE FROM GODLY VALUES

Although there have been attempts to distance us from godly hallmarks throughout our history, I believe our first truly serious departure was due to the U.S. Supreme Court's 1948 decision in *McCollum v. Board of Education,* about the interaction between government and religion. The issue arose because several faith-based groups—including those from the Protestant, Jewish, and Roman Catholic churches—were offering voluntary courses about their beliefs on school property during usual hours of operation.

Although the students were required to have written approval from their parents and no cost was incurred by the school board for the lessons, the Supreme Court found, "This is beyond all question a utilization of the tax-established and tax-supported public school system to aid religious groups to spread their faith. And it falls squarely under the ban of the First Amendment" [333 U.S. 203].

It is interesting that the court focused on the "ban" of the First Amendment, considering that this provision in our Bill of Rights doesn't even use that word but rather states:

Congress shall make no law respecting an establishment of religion, or prohibiting the free exercise thereof; or abridging the freedom of speech, or of the press; or the right of the people peaceably to assemble, and to petition the government for a redress of grievances.

The Intent of Our Founding Fathers

Although the Founders intended for the First Amendment to limit the *government's* reach, the court distorted the law. They said, in essence, that if the authorities could not offer classrooms to *all* religions, they could not offer time or space to any faith [330 U.S. 1; 333 U.S. 203].

Nothing could be further from the principles instituted by those who framed the Constitution. Why do I think so? Because I have studied history.

Our Founding Fathers upheld citizens' rights to worship where and when they pleased. They simply did not want to impose a national religion on the people because they understood the difficulties a state church could create. Allow me to explain.

> Our Founding Fathers upheld citizens' rights to worship where and when they pleased.

Christian Roots Across the Sea

You've most likely heard of one of England's most famous monarchs, King Henry VIII, who reigned from 1509 until his death in 1547. Henry famously broke with the Roman Catholic Church because he wanted to annul his marriage to Catherine of Aragon—who was unable to give him a male heir.

In 1534, Henry was declared Supreme Head of the Church of England, and assumed the responsibility of the nation's spiritual direction; this declaration positioned the land's monarchs as Head of the Church for centuries to come. In fact, sovereigns to this day are given the title of "Defender of the Faith and Supreme Governor of the Church of England"—a heavy-duty title, indeed.

Thus began several decades of targeted religious persecution. In order to show Henry's dominance over the Roman Catholic Church, he had the majority of monasteries and religious houses dissolved, their lands transferred to the crown, and many of their leaders executed.

Later, in an effort to reverse her father's reforms and restore Catholicism as the national religion, Mary I—also known as "Bloody Mary"—had almost three hundred Protestant believers burned at the stake, and more than eight hundred others fled the country.

The persecution did not stop there. The struggle between Catholics and Protestants continued—as did the harassment of whichever faith was out of power. England experienced the mass exodus of Puritans, Baptists, Quakers, Catholics, Separatists, and many other denominations to the New World in the hope of finding a place to worship as they pleased.

Religious intolerance was rampant in other places as well—such as discrimination against the Mennonites in Switzerland, the Huguenots in France, and the Anabaptists in Germany, among many others.

FAILURE #2: A PERVERSION OF THE FOUNDING FATHERS' INTENT

The religious intolerance of England is why the Founding Fathers made it very clear that government was to refrain from establishing and defending a particular church, because it could ultimately result in the persecution and execution of citizens.

Did this mean that the Founders didn't want any mention of religion in our public institutions? Absolutely not! The framers of the Constitution were all in favor of individuals expressing their religious viewpoints and having the liberty to establish the churches they wanted. They saw a true faith in God as foundational to the success of the aspiring republic.

In fact, the father of our country

> The Founders saw a true faith in God as foundational to the success of the aspiring republic.

and its first president, George Washington, confirms, "While just government protects all in their religious rights, true religion affords to government its surest support."

A Dividing Wall, but for Whose Protection?

You may be wondering why political commentators and legal experts are always focusing on the division between faith and government. Let us note for the record that nothing in the U.S. Constitution establishes a "separation of church and state." That wording comes from a letter from Thomas Jefferson penned in 1802 to the Danbury Baptist Association. The following is a selection from Jefferson's letter:

> *Believing with you that religion is a matter which lies solely between Man and his God, that* he owes account to none other for his faith or his worship, that the legitimate powers of government reach actions only, and not opinions, *I contemplate with sovereign reverence that act of the whole American people which declared that their legislature should* "make no law respecting an establishment of religion, or prohibiting the free exercise thereof," *thus building a wall of separation between Church & State. Adhering to this expression of the supreme will of the nation in behalf of the rights of conscience,* I shall see with sincere satisfaction the progress of those sentiments which tend to restore to man all his natural rights, convinced he has no natural right in opposition to his social duties. *(Roman type used for emphasis; quoted phrase is from the First Amendment to the Bill of Rights)*

What issue were the Danbury Baptists addressing? Their concern was that the First Amendment was attempting to ensure freedom of religion, which is something only God can really do. If the government thought itself the arbiter or grantor of religious freedom—giving and taking it away as it pleased—their right to worship the Lord could then be impeded by lawmakers. They wrote:

Such has been our laws and usages, and such still are, that Religion is considered as the first object of Legislation, and therefore what religious privileges we enjoy (as a minor part of the State) we enjoy as favors granted, and not as inalienable rights. And these favors we receive at the expense of such degrading acknowledgments, as are inconsistent with the rights of freemen. It is not to be wondered at therefore, if those who seek after power and gain, under the pretense of government and Religion, should reproach their fellow men, *should reproach their Chief Magistrate, as an enemy of religion, law, and good order, because he will not, dares not, assume the prerogative of Jehovah and make laws to govern the Kingdom of Christ. (Roman added for emphasis.)*

As Defender of the Faith and Supreme Governor of the Church of England, Henry VIII and Mary I believed they could express their authority over the beliefs of others, and used their power to persecute those who disagreed with them. Conceivably, our Founding Fathers contended, the United States could fall into the same trap as well.

But Jefferson assured the Danbury Baptists it would not. The wall of separation he spoke of was *to protect the church, not the state*. The Constitution's purpose was to safeguard the rights of individuals against tyrants.

Yet Jefferson did not believe this meant that leaders had to repress their devotion in God to be public servants. Notice the concluding sentence of Jefferson's earlier quote. He believed

> "Where the Spirit of the Lord is, there is liberty."
> —2 Corinthians 3:17

"man . . . has no natural right in opposition to his social duties." That means that a person's faith in the Lord would in no way impede his ability to govern.

For Those Yearning to Breathe Free

I believe that the faith of our Founding Fathers is the reason that the United States continues to be a safe harbor and bastion of freedom for those who have been oppressed throughout the world. Second Corinthians 3:17 affirms, "Where the Spirit of the Lord is, there is liberty."

For more than two hundred years after the Constitution was penned, America has been openly described as a "Christian nation." This was not because the government of the United States declared itself to be so, but because many of its people have been believers—they have attended Christ-centered churches, held biblical values, and identified themselves as blood-bought followers of Jesus.

Interestingly, this has never deterred individuals of other faiths from coming to this country. On the contrary, immigrants understood that their own values would be allowed and protected under the broad umbrella of religious and political liberty. The autonomy to worship as one pleased was extended to everyone, regardless of their beliefs.

FAILURE #3: A REVISED UNDERSTANDING OF CHOICE

Sadly, the freedom that began as the great strength of our nation has been so distorted that it has actually begun to undermine its very foundation. Whereas the Declaration of Independence ensures "certain unalienable Rights"—which were enumerated as "Life, Liberty and the pursuit of Happiness"—some in our society have attempted to expand those privileges in ways our Founders never envisioned.

Often cloaked under the guise of "freedom of choice," there are those who think that every person can choose how he or she wants to live in society, without personal restriction or responsibility. It sounds good at first, until we understand the ramifications of what they are advocating, which at times includes the legalization of drugs, prostitution, and state-assisted homicide.

This is the very problem that Paul warned against when he wrote, "It was for freedom that Christ set us free; therefore keep standing firm and do not be subject again to a yoke of slavery. . . . You were called to freedom, brethren; only do not turn your freedom into an opportunity for the flesh, but through love serve one another" (Galatians 5:1, 13).

You and I understand that there are things that we may be at liberty to do which would actually lead us back into emotional, spiritual, and physical bondage. Paul explains it this way: "All things are lawful for me, but not all things are profitable. All things are lawful for me, but I will not be mastered by anything" (1 Corinthians 6:12). Can we do these things—can we push the boundaries of our freedoms and come up with reasons that appear reasonable and even humane for practicing them? Theoretically, yes. Should we? Absolutely not!

> There are things that we may be at liberty to do which would actually lead us back into emotional, spiritual, and physical bondage.

Of course, those who would exploit the freedoms that the Constitution ensures are sometimes quick to tell others to mind their own business. In other words, they will tell us how we should speak and live, and demand that we accept behavior that contradicts God's Word. They insist that we never disagree with their choices—even though we only do so out of loving concern for their souls and safety.

The idea of "freedom of choice" is actually misleading, because in reality, no one has total liberty in deciding their course or future. We are governed not only by community, state, and national regulations but also by the laws of nature and societal norms. I think that reasonable people will also agree that our freedoms should not cause harm to others.

Likewise, there is another limit to our autonomy—we are ultimately accountable to God. Whether we acknowledge His authority over our lives or not, the Father establishes boundaries in His Word for our safety:

"You shall not murder" (Exodus 20:13).
"You shall not steal" (Exodus 20:15).
"You shall not bear false witness" (Exodus 20:16).

And so forth. The Lord's commandments limit our personal liberties, but they do so for our good. In the end, the only choice we're truly free to make is whether we will obey the Father or not.

FAILURE #4: A REVISED BELIEF ABOUT GOD'S INVOLVEMENT

Sadly, the Lord is often excluded when considering practical, economic, or political issues. The prevailing sentiment seems to be, "God has nothing to do with our public policy." This way of thinking shows the influence of secular humanism on our society—the belief that people can do ethical and moral good without the Lord's input.

We can see this in the way many frame discussions about our nation's origins and Constitution. In fact, a number of years ago, I came across a 1908 edition of a magazine published by an atheist. It made these claims:

- "This nation was not founded upon God."

- "This nation was not founded upon Scriptural principles."

- "This nation was not founded by godly men."

- "There's no evidence of anything biblical in the founding of this nation."

Then the author stated, "The atheists of the United States must rise to a realization that the symbol of prayer is powerful enough to return the nation to a theocratic type of government which was everywhere apparent in the original colonies."

I found it interesting that this publisher held prayer in such high regard—especially given his refusal to acknowledge the Lord's existence.

Schools Without Prayer or Bible

What is not so amusing is the devastating effect this destructive belief system has had on our country. After the 1948 *McCollum v. Board of Education* ruling that prohibited religious instruction in public schools, there were several court decisions that continued to limit public prayer and Bible reading, such as these:

- *Tudor v. Board of Education* in 1954—The Supreme Court affirmed a lower-court decision that outside groups such as the Gideons could not distribute free Bibles to willing recipients through channels such as the public schools [100 A.2d 857].

- *Engel v. Vitale* in 1962—The Supreme Court ruled that reciting the nondenominational Regents' prayer each morning in the schools was unconstitutional, even though students who objected to the practice were excused [370 U.S. 421].

- *Murray v. Curlett* and *Abington Township School District v. Schempp* in 1963—The Supreme Court combined these two lower-court cases and declared recitations of the Bible and the Lord's Prayer in schools unconstitutional [374 U.S. 203].

As you can imagine, there have been more legal challenges since then, but the major damage had already been done. The ban on prayer and the reading of God's Word in schools has not only weakened our children's understanding of authority and accountability but it has also led to a distortion of our country's history. Our children today have little understanding about the Bible and how the Founders framed our laws and our national traditions according to scriptural principles.

Testimonies from History

Did you know that our Founding Fathers and other key leaders in our country said the following things about the Bible and their faith in the Lord?

- In 1620, those who signed on to the Mayflower Compact sealed the agreement with these words, "In the name of God, by the grace of God, to the glory of God, and the advancement of Christian faith."

- Our first president, George Washington, said, "It is impossible to rightly govern the world without the Bible and God."

- Our seventh president, Andrew Jackson, affirmed, "That Book [referring to the Bible], Sir, is the rock on which our Republic rests."

- Our sixteenth president, Abraham Lincoln, wrote, "I believe the Bible is the best gift that God has ever given to man. All the good from the Savior of the world is communicated to us through this Book. I have been driven many times to my knees by the overwhelming conviction that I had nowhere else to go."

- Our twenty-fifth president, William McKinley, said, "The more profoundly we study this wonderful Book and the more closely we observe its divine precepts, the better citizens we will become and the higher will be our destiny as a nation."

- Our fortieth president, Ronald Reagan, declared, "Within the covers of the Bible are all the answers for all the problems men face. The Bible can touch hearts, order minds, and refresh souls."

- Noah Webster, originator of the most popular dictionary in America, wrote in 1832: "The principles of all genuine liberty and of wise laws and administrations are to be drawn from the Bible, and sustained by its authority. The man, therefore, who wakens or destroys the divine authority of that Book may be accessory to all the public disorders which society is doomed to suffer."

- A few years later, in 1848, Representative Robert C. Winthrop, Speaker of the House during the thirtieth Congress, said: "All societies of men must be governed in some way or other. Men in ordering words must be controlled either by a power within or a power without. Either by the Word of God or by the strong arm of man. Either by the Bible or by the bayonet."

- Horace Greeley, founding editor of the *New York Tribune* and presidential candidate in 1872, went so far as to say, "It is impossible, either physically or mentally, to enslave a Bible-reading people. The principles of the Bible are the groundwork of human freedom."

Of course, there are many more references than we can mention here. However, I pray you see the truth that the Founders of our nation *did* believe in God. They were not all Christians; in fact, two of the most famous of our founders were Unitarians.

They all believed that a Republic founded on devotion to God was much stronger than one with no faith at all.

But they were all men of prayer, and many wrote and spoke very pro-lifically and powerfully about matters of faith.

They all believed that a Republic founded on devotion to God was much stronger than one with no faith at all.

FAILURE #5: A DISRESPECT FOR ALMIGHTY GOD

As I mentioned earlier, the court rulings against prayer and Scripture reading in the schools not only opened the door for the re-writing of American history but also resulted in a loss of respect for Almighty God. Remember the wisdom of Proverbs 29:18: "Where there is no vision, the people are unrestrained." Or, as the *Living Bible* phrases it, "Where there is ignorance of God, the people run wild."

In other words, without a palpable reminder of the Lord's presence, people forget that they are accountable to Him, that their actions have both immediate and eternal consequences. Proverbs 10:27 warns, "The fear of the LORD prolongs life, but the years of the wicked will be shortened."

But what, you may ask, is there to be gained if people are afraid of God? When Scripture refers to "the fear of the LORD," it does not mean that people should be scared of the Father or live in constant terror of what He will do.

Rather, it indicates the attitude we should exhibit before Him, which is extreme awe at His holiness, majesty, and splendor. We bow down in humility before the Creator and King of all creation—the One who is omnipotent (all-powerful), omnipresent (always with us wherever we are, during every moment), omniscient (all-knowing and wise), and omni-benevolent (unconditional and perfect in His love for us).

Having a fear of the Lord—at its core—means having a heart

of worship and reverence for God and His Word. It leads to the stability, success, preservation, and well-being of individuals and nations.

Personal Benefits from a Healthy Respect for God

Here is what the Bible says are some of the many benefits of a healthy respect for the Father:

- "The fear of the LORD is clean, enduring forever; the judgments of the LORD are true; they are righteous altogether. . . . by them Your servant is warned; in keeping them there is great reward" (Psalm 19:9, 11).

- "The fear of the LORD is the beginning of wisdom; a good understanding have all those who do His commandments" (Psalm 111:10).

- "The fear of the LORD is the beginning of knowledge" (Proverbs 1:7).

- "In the fear of the LORD there is strong confidence, and his children will have refuge" (Proverbs 14:26).

- "The fear of the LORD is a fountain of life, that one may avoid the snares of death" (Proverbs 14:27).

- "Better is a little with the fear of the LORD than great treasure and turmoil with it" (Proverbs 15:16).

- "By lovingkindness and truth iniquity is atoned for, and by the fear of the LORD one keeps away from evil. When a man's ways are pleasing to the LORD, He makes even his enemies to be at peace with him" (Proverbs 16:6–7).

- "The fear of the LORD leads to life, so that one may sleep satisfied, untouched by evil" (Proverbs 19:23).

- "The reward of humility and the fear of the LORD are riches, honor and life" (Proverbs 22:4).

- "Do not let your heart envy sinners, but live in the fear of the LORD always. Surely there is a future, and your hope will not be cut off" (Proverbs 23:17–18).

National Benefits from a Healthy Respect for God

A strong and vigorous respect for the Father is absolutely crucial for our success as a country. Think about it. Our Forefathers served God and He blessed their faithfulness.

> Having a fear of the Lord—at its core—means having a heart of worship and reverence for God and His Word.

If the Lord had not sustained the early settlers through those extremely difficult years, they wouldn't have made it. It is a miracle that they survived. It is also extraordinary that they eventually united themselves, declared their independence, won a hard-fought war against a vastly superior military, and were able to construct a system of government that has continued to flourish for more than two hundred years.

Why have we been so favored by the Father? I believe the answer is threefold:

1. We are a bastion of freedom in the world. When the United States was founded, it was unlike anything anyone had ever seen before. Never throughout world history had there been a country *of, by, and for the people,* a country that had *such liberty for and confidence in the common man.* This was because the Founders were believers—men who understood the life-changing influence the Savior could have upon each person. Whereas many other nations have been established on the notion that the people could not govern themselves and must be controlled, the United States was different. It protected the autonomy and self-determination of each citizen.

This is why individual human rights are so important and why so many immigrants have found a better life here. They are no longer trapped by social and economic systems that were created to keep them in some arbitrary, predetermined class.

2. We are a very generous nation. The United States has also been known for its philanthropic spirit, with citizens voluntarily giving in excess of $300 billion in charitable contributions each year. Whenever disasters strike around the world—such as the 2010 earthquake in Haiti or the 2011 tsunami in Japan—Americans have been quick to offer assistance and relief.

3. We are a country that has devoted itself to spreading the gospel around the world. More evangelistic efforts have been launched by or funded by Americans than by any other people in history—past or present. In fact, 85 percent of resources given to missions come from the United States. That doesn't mean that the majority of missionaries in the world are Americans—but that many of the contributions that enable the proclamation of the gospel worldwide come from our country.

FAILURE #6: A RELIANCE ON SECULAR HUMANISM

I believe America is the greatest nation on earth because of the three factors identified above; we are a bastion of liberty, we are generous and compassionate both at home and abroad, and we stand for the gospel. In other words, the Lord has blessed us because we have honored Him.

Of course, this places us in direct opposition to the enemy of our souls, whose goal is to demoralize believers and stop them from preaching the truth of salvation through Jesus Christ. Therefore, there are influences we should be aware of—and pitfalls we should look out for—that directly impact our ability to remain a strong witness for Christ around the world.

The first of those pitfalls is *secular humanism.* As we discussed before, this is the belief that people can do ethical and moral good without God's input. It weakens our understanding of authority and accountability and also leads to a distortion of our country's history.

The second pitfall is *increasing taxation.* When our lawmakers tax us beyond all reason, resources that could otherwise be used to fund church and mission work diminish.

These two factors work together. You see, the fabrication that we are no longer a Christian nation stems from the destructive philosophy of secular humanism. In essence, the citizenry is told it no longer needs the Lord, that mankind can best choose what is right and wrong. Then, when the people truly require help, the government comes to the rescue. Because of the greatness of the need, taxation rises, and our bondage to and dependence upon the ruling authorities increases.

We become progressively less able to carry out the commission Christ gave to us: "Go therefore and make disciples of all the nations, baptizing them in the name of the Father and the Son and the Holy Spirit, teaching them to observe all that I commanded you" (Matthew 28:19–20).

This is why we must not allow the vocal few or unreasonable lawsuits to define who we are as Americans. The United States *is* a Christian nation. We may not always act as Christ-like as we should, but that does not change the fact that this country was established on the immu-

The United States *is* a Christian nation.

table principles of the Word of God. We can and should strive to honor the Lord once again.

DECISIONS MADE TODAY IMPACT OUR TOMORROW

It is imperative that we change the course of this nation now. If we don't, we are headed for a terrible tragedy. Proverbs 14:12 warns, "There is a way which seems right to a man, But its end is the way of death." Those who feel that we do not need God and that government is the answer to all our troubles may mean well. But they are driving us toward utter disaster.

What you and I do—the decisions we make and the way we choose to live—has a greater impact on those around us than we may realize. Like a stone tossed into a pond, which creates radiating circles that go all the way to the edges of the water, our influence can positively affect our communities, cities, states, nation, and the world. Our faithfulness to God and stand for our nation *can* make a difference for our children, grandchildren, and for the generations to come.

The choice is ours. However, we should not imagine that we can merely opt out of making a decision. We cannot just put off standing for what is right. To do so is to be culpable of allowing the downfall of our nation.

The Lord told the prophet Ezekiel, "I searched for a man among them who would build up the wall and stand in the gap before Me for the land, so that I would not destroy it; but I found no one. Thus I have poured out My indignation on them" (Ezekiel 22:30–31).

Will God find someone to "stand in the gap" for America, to pray for its citizens and be an example of His love and righteousness to the nation?

A Harvest Regardless

Our choices—or the refusal to make them—have consequences. We are never correct in concluding that we can do anything we want as long as we believe in Jesus Christ as our Savior. Far from it! The apostle Paul wrote "Do not be deceived, God is not mocked; for whatever a man sows, this he will also reap. For the one who sows to his own flesh will from the flesh reap corruption, but the one who sows to the Spirit will from the Spirit reap eternal life" (Galatians 6:7–8).

Because of the salvation we enjoy and the knowledge of God we have as Christians, we have an even greater responsibility: first, for our nation's future; and second, for the salvation of our fellow citizens. We must be found faithful.

Sadly, the truth of the matter is that we have been complacent much too long, allowing those who oppose Christ to have far too free a reign. We have remained silent as they have planted the seeds of the sinful nature; and we are now seeing the terrible yield. As I have often said:

> *We reap what we sow,*
> *more than we sow,*
> *and later than we sow.*

Any farmer understands this principle, it is as fixed and sure as any of the other laws of nature. If we plant tomato seeds in the ground, it's because we expect to grow tomatoes. We will harvest the product of the kind of seed we have placed in the ground.

Therefore, when we wonder at the immorality in our country, we must ask whether we as Christians have sown righteousness as we have been commanded.

When we complain because of the lack of education in our nation, we must consider whether the church has been consistent in teaching biblical truth and leading others into a growing relationship with Jesus Christ.

And when we weep because God is no longer honored in our land, we must examine ourselves—whether we have humbled ourselves before the Father as we should. Have we fallen to our knees in repentance and prayed for the lost souls of our fellow citizens?

Jesus taught:

"You will know them by their fruits. Grapes are not gathered from thorn bushes nor figs from thistles, are they? So every good tree bears good fruit, but the bad tree bears bad fruit. A good tree cannot produce bad fruit, nor can a bad tree produce good fruit. Every tree that does not bear good fruit is cut down and thrown into the fire. So then, you will know them by their fruits." (Matthew 7:16–20)

Friend, we cannot allow sin to run rampant in the church and expect the rest of the country to grow in godliness. Life simply does not work that way. As we read in 1 Peter 4:17, "It is time for judgment to begin with the household of God."

We must begin with our own hearts and church families. In order to turn the tide, we must pull up those roots of rebellion in our own backyard.

> We cannot allow sin to run rampant in the church and expect the rest of the country to grow in godliness.

The Turning That Is Required

It is not easy to stand against secular humanism, but it is necessary. The confessions we utter, the repentance we pursue, the prayers we voice, the votes we cast, the difficult stands we take, and all the seeds we sow in righteousness today will produce the harvest we experience tomorrow. Yes, there will be opposition. This is why the apostle Paul writes, "Let us not lose heart in doing good, for in due time we will reap if we do not grow weary" (Galatians 6:9). God will honor all you do in obedience to Him.

The psalmist affirmed: "The LORD loves justice and does not forsake His godly ones; they are preserved forever, but the descendants of the wicked will be cut off" (Psalm 37:28).

Therefore, let us clear out the ungodliness that has taken root in our nation, starting with our own hearts. And let's plant the seeds of truth, just as our Founders did. We can and should take stock of the past and begin furrowing the path to where we want to go as a country—back in line with the Father's will and for His glory.

It's difficult, but not unattainable. After all, with God, *all things* are possible.

Help us, Lord, to get back on track and to
return to the purposes
You planned for us as a nation.
Rekindle in us a desire for the freedoms and
responsibilities you gave to our Forefathers.
Renew righteousness in us,
individually and as a nation.

HOW *YOU* CAN HELP TURN THE TIDE

1. *"Studying the past helps us to know what we wish to become; it clarifies where we have been and where we have gone astray."*

What did you learn from Dr. Stanley's overview of the past—or from your own studies of the past—that can help you as you try to influence our great country?

2. *"We should not imagine that we can merely opt out of making a decision. We cannot just put off standing for what is right."*

After reading Dr. Stanley's statement above, what decisions can you make that will enable you to stand up for what is right?

3. Dr. Stanley shares this convicting statement: *"When we weep because God is no longer honored in our land, we must examine ourselves—whether we have humbled ourselves before the Father as we should. Have we fallen to our knees in repentance and prayed for the lost souls of our fellow citizens?"*

Ask God to help you examine your own heart (read Psalm 139:23–24). Look at your practices: Have you fallen to your knees in repentance and prayed for your lost fellow citizens? How can you implement changes in your life in order to help turn the tide?

CHAPTER 4

THE ECONOMIC TSUNAMI

The Intertwining of Debt, Overtaxation, and Unemployment

As I mentioned in the opening paragraphs of this book, the tremendous damage from storms and destructive tides can be overwhelming. We witnessed this in the unprecedented flooding in Australia in 2011, and also in Nashville, Tennessee, in 2010. It seems that very little is left standing once the raging waters hit.

The same is true when it comes to the tidal wave assailing our nation's economy—which is comprised of:

- escalating debt.

- increasing taxation.

- and rising unemployment.

When these three forces are intertwined, devastation is sure to follow.

THE GROWING STORM OF *DEBT*

The first factor we will examine is our mounting debt. According to Alan Krueger, chief economist and assistant secretary of the Treasury Department from 2009 to 2010, net household wealth has been reduced by approximately $17 trillion because of this economic downturn and rising indebtedness. This is money that Americans no longer have to provide for the needs of our families and communities.

In addition to the indebtedness and decreased income of individual households, our nation is accumulating alarming debt. There are several Internet sites that calculate our national indebtedness in real time.* As I write this chapter, I can see that we owe more than $14 trillion, and that number is rising every second. On December 31, 2009—roughly a year ago—the figure stood at just over $12.3 trillion. The escalation is absolutely astounding.

I can scarcely fathom the concept of "trillion," and I know I'm not alone. What does resonate is that the United States is amassing debt at the rate of $3.87 billion *a day*. That means that if every citizen were to pay an equal part of what the U.S. owes at the time of this writing, each one would be responsible for approximately $45,000. Distributed only among actual taxpayers, the bill would nearly triple, with each one owing more than $125,000.

Who will pay this debt? You may not be all that concerned about that right now. You may think, *Well, no one has handed me a bill— what does it really matter?* Yet the responsibility to reimburse this money hangs over all of us, threatening to bankrupt our nation. Someone will be required to repay it—and it may very well be our children or grandchildren. Even worse, a foreign power may find itself in the position to claim ownership of the country we love—and

---

* You can see the debt accumulate at sites such as www.usdebtclock.org/.

we may be in danger of losing the lifestyle and freedoms to which we have become accustomed (see Habakkuk 2:7).

We tend to look at the financially struggling countries in Europe and shake our heads in pity for their plight. It was not so long ago that Greece, Spain, Portugal, Ireland, and other nations were flourishing. Yet now they are facing bankruptcy. And when a nation becomes insolvent, its citizens lose their freedom. Someone else gains control.

To think that the United States could not find itself in the same position is at best naïve and at worst arrogant.

This is why God's Word warns, "The borrower becomes the lender's slave" (Proverbs 22:7). The Lord could not be clearer: *do not borrow*. In fact, the apostle Paul likewise admonishes, "Owe nothing to anyone except to love one another" (Romans 13:8).

> "The borrower becomes the lender's slave."—Proverbs 22:7

"But," someone may argue, "the U.S. *needed* that money to pay for our recovery from natural disasters, the terrorist attacks, and the bad decisions made by our banking, real estate, and manufacturing industries. That expense was unavoidable."

Is this really true? Was all of that additional funding, in fact, necessary?

Many disagree that more spending was what was required, and I am one of them. When individuals or companies have financial difficulties, they do well to reevaluate their budgets, cut wastefulness, and decrease expenditures. Our government has done just the opposite—which only deepens our problems.

THE EXPANDING STORM OF *TAXATION*

The truth of the matter is that our government needs to reduce spending. If you are an average taxpayer, you work almost four months a year just to pay the charges and tariffs required by law.

Of course, some of these monies are applied to very important and valuable initiatives such as our local and national defense and our nation's infrastructure. It is right that our taxes be spent on such things because—as I said in the first chapter—it is the government's responsibility to protect us. This obligation is enumerated in the Preamble of our Constitution:

> *We the People of the United States, in Order to form a more perfect Union, establish Justice, insure domestic Tranquility, provide for the common defense, promote the general Welfare, and secure the Blessings of Liberty to ourselves and our Posterity, do ordain and establish this Constitution for the United States of America.*

Now, there may be some people wondering what the term *welfare* is doing in the Preamble of the Constitution. Is this where the idea of our current entitlement system comes from? Is it the government's responsibility to take care of us?

The answer to that is no. Remember, the meaning of expressions can change over time, and for the Founders, the term *welfare* meant the "general well-being" of the citizenry. Their intention was never to take the resources of one individual in order to fulfill the needs of another.

Colonel David Crockett (Davy Crockett, as many came to know him), a representative from Tennessee, voiced this principle when he said, "We have the right as individuals, to give away as much of our own money as we please in charity; but as members of Congress we have no right to appropriate a dollar of the public money [to charity]."

Likewise, President Grover Cleveland affirmed, "I will not be a party to stealing money from one group of citizens to give to another group of citizens, no matter what the need or apparent justification. Once the coffers of the federal government are open to the public, there will be no shutting them again."

How far we have come from that understanding. In the *Harvard Political Review*'s 2010 "Annual Report of the United Stated of

America," Chris Danello reports, "The CBO [Congressional Budget Office] estimates that in ten years entitlement spending will reach 22 percent of GDP [Gross Domestic Product], about as much as the federal government spends on the entire budget today."

We have progressed from entitlement spending having no place in the country's budget to slowly taking it over completely.

Does this mean we should stop paying our taxes? Absolutely not. We are still called to be examples of good citizenship. The apostle Paul wrote: "Render to all what is due them: tax to whom tax is due; custom to whom custom; fear to whom fear; honor to whom honor" (Romans 13:7).

> **We have progressed from entitlement spending having no place in the country's budget to slowly taking it over completely.**

Likewise, when Jesus was confronted by opponents who tried to trick Him into saying that men should not pay their taxes to oppressive rulers, His answer was clearly on the side of good citizenship:

> *They [the religious leaders] sent their disciples to Him [Jesus], along with the Herodians, saying, "Teacher, we know that You are truthful and teach the way of God in truth, and defer to no one; for You are not partial to any. Tell us then, what do You think? Is it lawful to give a poll-tax to Caesar, or not?" But Jesus perceived their malice, and said, "Why are you testing Me, you hypocrites? Show Me the coin used for the poll-tax." And they brought Him a denarius. And He said to them, "Whose likeness and inscription is this?" They said to Him, "Caesar's." Then He said to them, "Then render to Caesar the things that are Caesar's; and to God the things that are God's." (Matthew 22:16–21)*

I would never tell you to ignore your duties—that would be absolutely contrary to what Jesus taught us. However, I do encourage you to become active in your opposition to rising taxes in our nation and to advocate for tax reform.

God has blessed Americans with the great privilege of liberty to voice our opinions in the issues of public policy—a freedom that not even the disciples were able to enjoy. And as I said in chapter 3, the more we pay in tariffs, the less we have to give to the proclamation of the gospel and the work of the church. We have a right and a responsibility to stand up and make sure that what we work for is put to the best use possible.

THE INTENSIFYING STORM OF *UNEMPLOYMENT*

This leads us to the third part of the tremendous problem facing the country, which is the high rate of unemployment. In 2010, that number was 9.6 percent nationally, and this does not count those who have simply given up looking for jobs. In some states, it was approaching 15 percent.

The statisticians tell us that 44 percent of the people who are unemployed are hardworking people who have lost their jobs and have been without an income for more than twenty-seven weeks. These are people who want to work and who have the skills and abilities that make them employable, but simply are not able to find anyone who is hiring.

In addition to those who are jobless, there are millions of people in our nation who are *underemployed*—they are working at posts that pay far less than their previous occupations and are doing tasks for which they are overqualified. These people cannot find a job in their field.

This, of course, has a myriad of implications and impacts every area of our society. We see the results all around us:

• Individuals are losing their homes by the tens of thousands.

• Parents are no longer able to send their children to college.

- People are dipping into—and many are losing—their retirement funds.

- Small businesses are folding.

- Churches and charitable organizations are being forced to close.

The truth of the matter is that with fewer people able to support themselves, fewer individuals paying taxes, and decreased production, the United States is teetering on the edge of collapse. Something must stop us before we fall into an even more serious economic recession or depression.

> The truth of the matter is that . . . the United States is teetering on the edge of collapse. Something must stop us before we fall into an even more serious economic recession or depression.

With all of this in mind, it is no surprise that people are unhappy, dejected, and even angry. It is terribly discouraging when men and women want to work—to provide for the needs of their children and households—but cannot do so. A person's self-worth can take a major hit—especially when one cannot even afford the basics of life. Eventually, the unemployed may give in to frustration, anger, sadness, and a sense of futility. Deep feelings of depression and anxiety take over.

That is why, at this point, I would like to take a moment to encourage those who are currently facing the devastating effects of unemployment.

Friend, if you are one of the many Americans who is out of work or facing terrible financial difficulties, *don't give up.* I know it is absolutely heartbreaking to be unable to take care of your family. The pressure associated with not having an income or being in danger of losing your house is immense. But God is your confidence in these troublesome times. He says,

You whom I have taken from the ends of the earth, and called from its remotest parts and said to you, "You are My servant, I have chosen you and not rejected you. Do not fear, for I am with you; do not anxiously look about you, for I am your God. I will strengthen you, surely I will help you, surely I will uphold you with My righteous right hand." (Isaiah 41:9–10)

Your life is still in His hands—regardless of what the economy is doing. Yes, this is a disheartening season. But as I often say, *disappointments in life are inevitable, but discouragement is a choice.* You do not have to give in to despair. This is not the end for you. Things can and will change for the better, but you must hold on to your faith in the Lord God. He works on behalf of those who wait for Him (see Isaiah 64:4). So trust Him, seek Him, and obey Him. He will be faithful to you.

> Things can and will change for the better, but you must hold on to your faith in the Lord God.

TAKING RESPONSIBILITY

That said, I believe that there is a way out of our financial difficulty that does not entail borrowing or increased taxation. However, we must search our hearts. We must begin by being willing to admit that we—as a country and as a culture—have a problem.

Part of what plagues our nation is our focus on material wealth. Because of our prosperity, we have grown somewhat comfortable and self-serving, and we've lost much of our understanding as to what is really important.

In most cases, we have more than sufficient resources for ourselves and our families. Sadly, many have come to believe that to be someone significant in this world, there are critical items to own, essential levels of wealth and notoriety to attain. We crave the latest, newest, and best gadgets, vehicles, and appliances. And we've fallen for the deceptive media messages that insist some things are absolutely indispensible to our lives, when, in reality, they may not be needed at all.

We need to understand that much of this material frenzy is feardriven. We are afraid of missing out, of not being good enough, of being judged, of not having the same opportunities as others. As a result, we rely on money as our source of worth and security, rather than our Savior, Jesus Christ. We fail to save for the future, choosing instead to acquire possessions, even to the point of putting ourselves and the nation into truly serious jeopardy.

Yet God's Word is clear: "He who trusts in his riches will fall, but the righteous will flourish like the green leaf" (Proverbs 11:28). In fact, Psalm 62:10–12 teaches us, "If riches increase, do not set your heart upon them. Once God has spoken; twice I have heard this: that power belongs to God; and lovingkindness is Yours, O Lord, for You recompense a man according to his work."

Friend, our value comes from our relationship with the Savior— not our portfolios of investments, our bank accounts, our salary levels, or what we own. Those things will fade away and fail us. Only intimacy with the Father gives us true worth or security (see Hebrews 13:5).

This does not mean I think we should buy only cheap products or hoard all of our money. I am all in favor of quality and buying the best I can. But I also prefer paying cash—saving until I can pay for an item, rather than putting it on a credit card.

I also believe that our first responsibility is to the Lord. Exodus 34:26 teaches, "You shall bring the very first of the first fruits of your soil into the house of the LORD your God." As believers, we must be faithful in giving our tithes and offerings, remembering that "it is He who is giving [us] power to make wealth" (Deuteronomy 8:18). We must also be devoted to one another and help those in need (Matthew 10:7–8; Romans 12; 2 Corinthians 9:6–8; James 2:15–17). Allow me to explain.

Somewhere along the line, many in our society—and also in our churches—have become convinced that it is the job of the government to help those who cannot care for themselves. They believe that their problems are someone else's responsibility.

Yet this is not what we find in Scripture. First John 3:16–18 admonishes:

> *We know love by this, that He laid down His life for us; and we ought to lay down our lives for the brethren. But whoever has the world's goods, and sees his brother in need and closes his heart against him, how does the love of God abide in him? Little children, let us not love with word or with tongue, but in deed and truth.*

In other words, it is individual *believers*—not the government—whom the Lord calls to minister to others and demonstrate the great love He has for them by providing for their needs. It is a *personal* responsibility—not one we can or should pass on to our elected officials or our national budget.

When we relinquish to federal bureaucracies the ability to help others, we also surrender very important opportunities to care for people's most critical spiritual need—their need for salvation.

Think about it: When we relinquish to federal bureaucracies the ability to help others, we also surrender very important opportunities to care for people's most critical spiritual need—their need for salvation. We give up an awesome chance to tell them about Jesus. This is a terrible shame, considering the hope that only He can provide.

THREE MISCONCEPTIONS ABOUT ECONOMIC MATTERS

From this misunderstanding of the government's role emerge three other major misconceptions in our national thinking about economic matters:

- *Misconception #1:* Our love for others is to be unconditional—and because love is best demonstrated by giving, we should therefore give unconditionally.

- *Misconception #2:* To fulfill our social responsibility, people who make more should pay a higher percentage in taxes, and those who require more should be given whatever they need.

- *Misconception #3:* With enough federal aid, we can end poverty.

Some may assume that the Bible teaches these things, but it does not. So we will look at these issues one at a time, understanding that for us to overcome our national difficulties, we must understand the truth.

Misconception #1: Our love for others is to be unconditional—and because love is best demonstrated by giving, we should therefore give unconditionally.

This line of reasoning sounds nice, but it is a distortion of truth. The Savior cares for all people and has given *everyone* an opportunity to come to Him, receive His mercy and forgiveness, and live in right relationship with Him. In fact, Romans 5:8 assures us, "God demonstrates His own love toward us, in that while we were yet sinners, Christ died for us." He offers His love to us without reservation or restriction.

However, the *benefits* of His love have a condition: we must *agree* to receive them. John 3:16 tells us, "God so loved the world, that He gave His only begotten Son, that *whoever believes in Him* shall not perish, but have eternal life." Notice the phrase in (the added) italics—not every person will experience salvation, only those *who believe in Jesus.*

The Lord loves us unconditionally, but we can choose not to accept His provision of forgiveness and be eternally separated from

Him. John 3:17–18 states, "God did not send the Son into the world to judge the world but that the world might be saved through Him. He who believes in Him is not judged; *he who does not believe has been judged already, because he has not believed* in the name of the only begotten Son of God." (Italics added for emphasis.)

Why is this? Remember the purpose for salvation—for the individual to have an intimate, personal relationship with the Lord (see John 17:3). If a person has no interest in God, then why would he or she wish to spend eternity with Him?

Now let us think of this in terms of giving. Jesus said:

> *Give to him who asks of you, and do not turn away from him who wants to borrow from you. You have heard that it was said, "You SHALL LOVE YOUR NEIGHBOR and hate your enemy." But I say to you, love your enemies and pray for those who persecute you, so that you may be sons of your Father who is in heaven. (Matthew 5:42–45)*

Why are we to be generous to others? So they can see the love of God in us and through us. We feed the hungry, clothe the naked, welcome the stranger, and visit the prisoner as if we were doing so for Christ Himself (see Matthew 25:34–45). And as we give, we teach in the hope that the recipients will come to know Jesus as their Savior.

However, there *is* a limit. There comes a point when giving to another person degenerates from ministry to dependency. They are neither growing closer to the Father nor respecting you. You are merely funding their irresponsible lifestyle. This is not biblical—not by a long shot.

Therefore, we are not to give unconditionally; we are to do so with wisdom and spiritual discernment.

Misconception #2: To fulfill our social responsibility, people who make more should pay a higher percentage in taxes, and those who require more should be given whatever they need.

Or, as Karl Marx put it, "From each according to his ability, to each according to his needs." The purpose for this, of course, is to redistribute the wealth of the nation. However, in terms of government, this unfortunately often degenerates into a lack of consequences for—and ultimately, the subsidizing of—irresponsible behavior. It is impossible to find any justification for this in Scripture.

On the contrary, in the parable of the talents, the servants who were faithful with what the master had given were rewarded, but the one who misused it was rebuked harshly (see Matthew 25:14–29). Jesus explained, "To everyone who has, more shall be given, and he will have an abundance; but from the one who does not have, even what he does have shall be taken away" (Matthew 25:29). Biblically, we are each charged to do and be our best—avoiding evil and obeying God.

Our system currently practices the exact opposite of the biblical standard—taking from those who are good stewards of their time and who use their talents successfully to give to those who do not. This is not only true of individuals but of corporations as well. How many conscientious, hardworking Americans and flourishing businesses were forced to fund the bailouts of so many irresponsible, failing companies? There is nothing biblical in this.

Misconception #3: With enough federal aid, we can end poverty.

Again, this sounds like a worthwhile pursuit. But over the years, the government has invested trillions of dollars in programs intended to provide for the poor and reduce their numbers. The War on Poverty, as it was called by the Johnson administration, set out to help the underprivileged by offering a myriad of progressive programs. Sadly, the only thing these initiatives achieved was to create successive generations of impoverished Americans. It proved that more government is never the answer—certainly not the biblical one—because it made the divisions between the economic classes even more apparent and antagonistic.

Scripture, of course, takes a very different view. James 2:1–6 admonishes:

> *My brethren, do not hold your faith in our glorious Lord Jesus Christ with an attitude of personal favoritism. For if a man comes into your assembly with a gold ring and dressed in fine clothes, and there also comes in a poor man in dirty clothes, and you pay special attention to the one who is wearing the fine clothes, and say, "You sit here in a good place," and you say to the poor man, "You stand over there, or sit down by my footstool," have you not made distinctions among yourselves, and become judges with evil motives? Listen, my beloved brethren: did not God choose the poor of this world to be rich in faith and heirs of the kingdom which He promised to those who love Him? But you have dishonored the poor man.*

The destitute and needy should always be welcome in our churches. We should love them and do our best to help them better their situations—teaching them the skills that will enable them to find work, guiding them in discovering all God created them to be, and demonstrating the godly disciplines that will lead them into a growing relationship with Jesus Christ.

With that said, I acknowledge that there are certainly those dear souls in our society who genuinely cannot support or care for themselves, and we as believers have a special responsibility to love and minister to them (see Deuteronomy 10:17–18; Proverbs 14:21; 19:17; 22:9; 29:7; and James 1:27). Just as Christ was compassionate toward such people, we should be also.

However, we should be firm with those who have simply become accustomed to a life of idleness and apathy. Even in the New Testament, there were those who constructed excuses as to why they could not be expected to labor. Many of the Christians in Thessalonica believed Jesus would return soon, so there was really no reason to work. But the apostle Paul was clear:

You yourselves know how you ought to follow our example, because we did not act in an undisciplined manner among you, nor did we eat anyone's bread without paying for it, but with labor and hardship we kept working night and day so that we would not be a burden to any of you; not because we do not have the right to this, but in order to offer ourselves as a model for you, so that you would follow our example. For even when we were with you, we used to give you this order: if anyone is not willing to work, then he is not to eat, either. For we hear that some among you are leading an undisciplined life, doing no work at all, but acting like busybodies. Now such persons we command and exhort in the Lord Jesus Christ to work in quiet fashion and eat their own bread. (2 Thessalonians 3:7–12)

EVERYONE CAN LEARN AND RESPONSIBLY CONTRIBUTE

The truth of the matter is that every person is capable of:

- learning more than he or she presently knows.

- acquiring at least one useful skill.

- doing some form of work that helps provide for his or her family or contributes to his or her community.

Let me add that we are also all capable of being taught, regardless of our age. If you can no longer find a use for your skill set, pursue a new one. It does not matter how old you are or how set in your ways you may have become; you can still gain knowledge of topics and talents that can make your life fuller and richer.

With very few exceptions, everyone can learn the information and skills necessary for self-sustenance. Some people may need more motivation, encouragement, inspiration, or assistance, but everyone can improve his or her situation and become an important and vibrant part of God's work in this world.

Of course, there may be those who disagree with me, wondering how much the disabled, mentally challenged, or emotionally wounded are able to do. Make no mistake, those individuals are very special in the Father's sight, and He has wonderful plans for them as well. In Psalm 139:13–16, David proclaims,

> *You formed my inward parts; You wove me in my mother's womb.*
> *I will give thanks to You, for I am fearfully and wonderfully*
> *made; wonderful are Your works, and my soul knows it very well.*
> *My frame was not hidden from You, when I was made in secret,*
> *and skillfully wrought in the depths of the earth; Your eyes have*
> *seen my unformed substance; and in Your book were all written*
> *the days that were ordained for me, when as yet there was not one*
> *of them.*

God has a plan for each and every person—regardless of nationality, background, abilities, or supposed hindrances. God forms each of us with awesome purposes in mind.

This is true of each and every person—regardless of nationality, background, abilities, or supposed hindrances. God forms each of us with awesome purposes in mind (see Ephesians 2:10).

Brokenness Is the Path to Maximum Usefulness

One of the most talented young men I've ever read about is a man who was born without arms or legs. He has achieved more than most people born without any physical limitations—graduating from college, writing books, traveling throughout the world to tell people about the gospel of Jesus Christ, and inspiring others to live a godly life.

Another very gifted individual I've had the privilege to read about lost his sight when he was in his twenties; he became totally and irreversibly blind. Despite his blindness, he has contributed to society and has done very well financially. He became a successful movie producer and won the top entertainment award in his field because of technology he developed to help the visually impaired enjoy what they are hearing on television.

What some view as their own disabilities, liabilities, and wounds are actually the stepping-stones God uses to teach them and help them succeed. While not everyone has the abilities these two young men have, our brokenness is still God's requirement for maximum usefulness. If we wish to be used by the Lord, we must first realize that we cannot succeed on our own. We must come to the point of acknowledging that He is our sufficiency and adequacy, and it is only in His power, wisdom, and love that we can achieve anything.

The apostle Paul understood this, which is why he wrote the following:

> To keep me from exalting myself, there was given me a thorn in the flesh, a messenger of Satan to torment me. . . . Concerning this I implored the Lord three times that it might leave me. And He has said to me, "My grace is sufficient for you, for power is perfected in weakness." Most gladly, therefore, I will rather boast about my weaknesses, so that the power of Christ may dwell in me. Therefore I am well content with weaknesses, with insults, with distresses,

with persecutions, with difficulties, for Christ's sake; for when I am weak, then I am strong. (2 Corinthians 12:7–10)

Paul understood that his own strength would need to decrease so that there would be absolutely no other explanation for his success than God's perfect wisdom and power. Everyone would have to recognize that it was the Lord who was demonstrating His awesome sufficiency in and through the apostle—and He would receive the glory.

Comforted to Become Comforters

Now, I know that some readers have been so seriously abused and mistreated that you wonder if the Lord can truly use you to help others and do great things for the sake of His name. Right now, you may even be thinking, *You don't understand my situation or how very difficult my life is. You couldn't possibly realize where I have been and the terrible things I have done.* You're correct, friend, I don't. But God does, and He absolutely loves you anyway.

But, you may say, *You have no concept of how I've been wronged or the loss I have experienced; you don't realize the emotional pain that keeps me from making progress.* Again, you're correct that I can't understand the specifics of your suffering, though I've experienced hurt and loss of my own. But God knows your unique wounds, and He offers you healing and hope. He can use you even as you experience trials. In fact, at times it is the difficulties of your life that He works through most powerfully.

The Father has not given up on you—so don't give up on Him. He still has a plan for your life, if you're willing to turn it over to Him. No matter how much you may have sinned or how you have been wounded by others, God can use you; He simply wants you to be His.

> The Father has not given up on you—so don't give up on Him.

Second Corinthians 1:4 tells us that the Lord "comforts us in all our affliction so that we will be able to comfort those who are in any affliction with the comfort with which we ourselves are comforted by God." In other words, there are other people out there who are just like you, and they also need to know that He loves them. You can have a very special ministry to them because you know just how they feel. Through all of your brokenness and because of what the Father has already done in your life, you've been uniquely equipped to console and counsel them in an awesome way.

If They Can, You Can

Age doesn't have to be a deterrent, either. Not long ago, I heard about an almost-ninety-year-old woman who regularly goes to what she calls an "old people's place." She plays the piano for the people who live there—lonely residents in their seventies and eighties who often live for months without having another visitor. They absolutely love her "piano ministry." It is her reason to get up every morning— the applause of the residents gives her a sense of worth and accomplishment. And her willingness to serve is a tremendous blessing to those who have the pleasure of hearing her.

Another man I know teaches a woodworking class to students from a very poor neighborhood. He is eighty-seven years old and instructs his pupils from a wheelchair. Some may think he has done enough and should retire. Yet nothing could make him give up the great satisfaction he feels as he watches those teenage boys learn a new skill. You see, most of those young men have been told that they will never amount to anything. They feel useless, helpless, and unwanted. But this man is transforming their lives—teaching them to think differently about themselves, training them in useful skills, and helping them achieve their goals for the future.

If these two souls can minister to others, you can as well. The point is using what you know to glorify God.

TRUSTING THE LORD
FOR ALL YOUR NEEDS

Now, it may seem that we have gotten a little off track. We began by talking about the economic tsunami our nation is facing, and are now discussing how you can be a blessing to those around you. You may be wondering how these two connect.

Perhaps the greatest key to our economic future lies in Christians once again believing God and being His ambassadors to the nation. Remember, our troubles are not really about money—there is a deeper spiritual concern here that we must acknowledge. The issue is really who or what we choose to rely on for our worth and security (see Matthew 6:19–24). First Timothy 6:9–12 reminds us:

> *Those who want to get rich fall into temptation and a snare and many foolish and harmful desires which plunge men into ruin and destruction. For the love of money is a root of all sorts of evil, and some by longing for it have wandered away from the faith and pierced themselves with many griefs. But flee from these things, you man of God, and pursue righteousness, godliness, faith, love, perseverance and gentleness. Fight the good fight of faith; take hold of the eternal life to which you were called, and you made the good confession in the presence of many witnesses.*

As believers, we will either serve the Lord or we will chase earthly security, which quickly fades. This is not to say we are to ignore our finances; rather, we are to honor God by being good stewards of them. However, we are also to pursue righteousness, godliness, faith, love, perseverance, gentleness—engaging in the good fight of faith so others will take hold of the eternal life.

In other words, our challenge is to again pick up the mantle that He gave to the church so long ago, which is to be His light to the world, in both word and deed, in the hope of leading others to salvation.

Therefore, friend, turn to God and ask Him how He desires to use you. He will show you how to minister to people's physical and emotional poverty so that you can tell them about how He fulfills their greatest spiritual need.

He will most certainly bless you as you obey Him, trust Him, and turn to Him for guidance.

Heavenly Father, please lead us out of debt.
Save us from the burden
of overtaxation. Put our nation back to work, Lord, and give
us a renewed understanding about our responsibilities
toward one another. Guide us in Your
love so that we can generously and faithfully lead others to You.
Free us to spread the Good News of Your salvation, mercy, and
forgiveness around the world so that others
will be saved and You will be glorified. Amen.

HOW *YOU* CAN HELP
TURN THE TIDE

1. *"'The borrower becomes the lender's slave' (Proverbs 22:7). . . . When individuals or companies have financial difficulties, they do well to reevaluate their budgets, cut wastefulness, and decrease expenditures."*

Dr. Stanley's statement above applies to both our individual lives and to our country. As you evaluate your own financial status, what do you need to do to reduce wastefulness and decrease expenditures? As we become more frugal individuals, we are better qualified to help turn the tide of our nation's unwise spending.

2. Dr. Stanley astutely says, *"I would never tell you to ignore your duties—that would be absolutely contrary to what Jesus taught us. However, I do encourage you to become active in your opposition to rising taxes in our nation and to advocate for tax reform."*

While behaving in a Christ-like manner, how can you become active in advocating for tax reform and speaking out against rising taxes?

3. *"When we relinquish to federal bureaucracies the ability to help others, we also surrender very important opportunities to care for people's most critical spiritual need—their need for salvation. We give up an awesome chance to tell them about Jesus."*

Even now you can exercise your freedom to help others and thus also address their most urgent spiritual need—that of knowing Jesus as their Savior. What can you do in your community to help others with their physical and emotional needs so that you can also help them with their spiritual needs? There is no more powerful way to turn the tide of our country than to bring lost souls to Jesus.

CHAPTER 5

THE DOWNWARD SPIRAL
OF SOCIALISM

Why the Government Is Not Our Keeper

For as long as I can remember, there have been calls to redistribute the wealth of our country—to nationalize businesses and make sure everyone receives his or her "fair share" of the American dream. But in recent years, the demands have increased—growing exponentially louder and angrier and promoting the cancer of class envy.

Have you ever wondered where these notions come from? Where is it stated in the laws of our land that assets must be evenly apportioned among all citizens?

Hopefully, you realize that these are not concepts established in our founding documents but symptoms of socialism destabilizing our representative republic. In fact, our Constitution has been enduring an onslaught from this destructive philosophy for more than 150 years.

SOCIALISM: A DEEP-SEATED PROBLEM

Some believe socialism is a fairly modern system—one that has existed in this nation for only the last fifty or sixty years. The truth of the matter is that the roots of this poisonous ideology can be traced back at least to the 1850s, perhaps even further.

During the mid- to late 1840s, there were terrible depressions and famines in places such as Germany due to failed crops, heavy taxation, cholera epidemics, and very difficult working conditions. Inspired by the February 1848 revolution in Paris, underprivileged German citizens rose up and demanded reforms—many of which were consistent with the socialist and communist tenets that were gaining traction at that time because they promised freedom from the misery people were experiencing. With the failure of many of these uprisings, however, many fled to the United States in the hope of finding a platform for their beliefs. They established clubs and societies by the 1850s for the purpose of spreading socialism in the states.

By 1874, the first organized political party—the Social Democratic Workingmen's Party of North America—was formed. By 1876, it would become the Socialist Labor Party of America, an organization that has run presidential nominees since 1892 and which continues to operate in our country to this day.

This very brief history shows that this devastating belief system has been undermining our national identity for a very long time. French philosopher and historian Alexis de Tocqueville, who lived through the revolutions of the mid-1800s, explained the vast disparity between the two political systems: "Democracy and socialism," he wrote, "have nothing in common but one word, equality. But notice the difference: while democracy seeks equality in liberty, socialism seeks equality in restraint and servitude."

> "While democracy seeks equality in liberty, socialism seeks equality in restraint and servitude."
> —Alexis de Tocqueville

THE DISASTROUS MISUNDERSTANDING
OF SOCIALISM

Unfortunately, I still meet individuals who have no real understanding of socialism or what it is doing to our country. Many of them believe it simply means the government will take care of the people.

However, *The Concise Encyclopedia of Economics* defines *socialism* as "a centrally planned economy in which the government controls all means of production and distribution." In other words, the *governing authorities*—not the people—decide what is fair and equitable. It makes the assumption that you and I are not capable to make the decisions necessary for our families; those in power must tell us what to do.

Consider how this differs from what the Founding Fathers originally intended for the United States to be: a *decentralized* federation of republics (the individual states), divided into three branches (executive, legislative, and judicial), which ensured freedom for the people from the control of the ruling class. The framers of the Constitution worked tirelessly, guaranteeing that the government would not become tyrannical and all-encompassing. They were even sensitive to the possibility of power being concentrated in the larger states, which was why the U.S. Senate was formed—making certain that the citizens of smaller states would have an equal voice in national issues.

When the Government Oversteps Its Bounds
Alexander Hamilton, one of the Founding Fathers and the first secretary of the Treasury, confirmed the dangers of government holding too much power, writing, "If the federal government should overpass the just bounds of its authority and make a tyrannical use of its powers, the people, whose creature it is, must appeal to the standard they have formed, and take such measures to redress the injury done to the Constitution as the exigency may suggest and prudence justify."

I believe this may be the reason our country's troubles have gotten so out of control: many of our citizens do not realize that the federal government is overstepping its bounds and that there are forces actively working against what our nation was originally founded to be.

Of course, part of the problem is that the stated goals of socialism *sound* so attractive—claiming to ensure the rights of the working class and the fair allocation of goods, services, and wealth. Its proponents point out the imbalances caused by capitalism and tell us how we can enjoy a more compassionate and equal existence. However, they do not tell us about the oppression, waste, corruption, and wretchedness that such a system brings.

A Philosophy of Failure

Winston Churchill, the prime minister who led the United Kingdom to victory during World War II, explained it well when he wrote, "Socialism is a philosophy of failure, the creed of ignorance, and the gospel of envy, its inherent virtue is the equal sharing of misery."

What Churchill was responding to and what we have witnessed throughout history is that socialism does not work because it is based on two faulty assumptions.

1. Socialism fails because it presumes an equal ability and desire among all people to work and manage resources. The main tenet of socialism is established on the flawed supposition that every person is laboring to the very best of his or her capability and is equally motivated to succeed. However, anyone who has spent any time working with others knows that this is not usually the case.

At one end of the spectrum are employees who will go above and beyond the call of duty—toiling to meet and surpass goals, accepting whatever challenges are offered to them, striving to accomplish great things, and doing their best because they perceive a higher purpose to their efforts. On the other end are workers who are not as motivated and do the least that they can to get by. For them, the job they do merely funds their personal objectives, and therefore, they expend the smallest amount of energy possible in their occupations.

The driving concept of socialism is that everyone will be more productive because all are working toward the same goal and receive the same compensation. But just the opposite is true. Because there is no reward for working harder, being creative, or using the gifts and talents God has given us—and there are also no consequences for poor performance—people do the least they can to get by. We see this now in government bureaucracies.

> Because there is no reward for working harder—and there are also no consequences for poor performance—people do the least they can to get by.

Socialism can never guarantee consistent input of talent and ability, and therefore, it cannot ensure equal productivity or output.

2. Socialism fails because it assumes that it can systematize decisions and equalize benefits. At the heart of socialism is also the assumption that there should be no private property—every person should have an equitable share of the total assets, with the government deciding what is appropriate. While this may be a nice idea, it simply does not work.

Take the single-payer government health-care system of Canada, for example. Although all citizens are, for the most part, guaranteed health care—which they are required to pay for in taxes—not every condition has approval for treatment. Because of the sluggish pace and interminable complexity of bureaucratic approvals, people often wait for months for crucial surgeries and therapies, which sometimes come too late to save them. Also, research and development of cures, procedures, and medications have been stifled because of the mismanagement and drain of resources from the national coffers.

The Canadian government simply cannot support the overwhelming demand or expense. Officials have done their best to regulate choices, but in the end, they have been unable to anticipate the unique circumstances each individual or family would face. Because of this, many citizens are forced to go to private clinics or travel to other countries for the life-saving treatments they need. They have realized that they cannot depend on the government to help them, so they save, get second and third jobs, and make the difficult sacrifices necessary in order to pay for the medical attention they require.

This goes to prove what I have often thought to be true—one can gather all the wealth of a nation and distribute it equally, but within a short span of time, the socioeconomic distinctions will reappear. Why? Because people inherently make choices about their money as it relates to their values: they save or spend based on their particular situations and what they believe.

Faith, dreams, goals, priorities, ambitions, abilities, and levels of energy define who people are—not their beginnings, and definitely not their possessions.

In other words, two people can commence from the same starting point, with similar benefits and assets, but still arrive at vastly different places. Their faith, dreams, goals, priorities, ambitions, abilities, and levels of energy define them—not their beginnings, and definitely not their possessions. The government simply cannot systematize or generalize who we are.

SOCIALISM STRIKES AT THE HEART OF HUMAN ASPIRATION

As you can imagine, with such a general, non-individual view of personhood, socialism eventually destroys a soul's hopes, dreams, and ingenuity. Scientific research studies show that people are often much less productive, efficient, creative, and concerned about the quality of the goods and services when they are under the oppression of a socialist government.

Likewise, people are more prone to absenteeism and demonstrate extreme apathy. In order to escape the pressures of their existence, there is frequently an abundance of addiction to drugs and alcohol, which consequently results in poorer health and greater friction within families. Suicides are also generally higher in socialist societies. For example, according to the World Health Organization (WHO), there is an average of 63.4 suicides per 100,000 people in the Russian Federation (which is still recovering from its many decades of enforced socialism). In the United States the average is much lower at 22.2 per 100,000.

I believe this is because socialism debases the three basic aspirations that reside in the heart of every man and woman:

- the desire to *be*—feeling acceptance and belonging.

- the yearning to *have*—achieving a sense of worth and love.

- the longing to *do*—attaining an understanding of one's own competency and security.

Although socialism *claims* to fulfill all of these needs, it actually impairs an individual's ability to realize them.

1. The Desire to *Be*

Proponents of socialism profess to give power to the helpless— asserting the rights of the working class. But in a true socialist society, a person can be only what the state says he or she can be. Children are assessed and told what career path they are permitted to pursue. This determines what role the child can fill in society— curtailing his or her creativity and initiative, and putting limits on what he or she can become.

When children are not allowed to discover the purpose for which God created them, they are unable to express who they truly are. Therefore, they cannot feel the acceptance and belonging they long to experience. Of course, as believers we realize this is something the Father offers to us freely. Romans 8:14–15 assures us, "All who are being led by the Spirit of God, these are sons of God. For you have not received a spirit of slavery leading to fear again, but you have received a spirit of adoption as sons."

In other words, while socialism hinders a person from becoming all he or she can be, our heavenly Father sets us free to reach our full potential. So we need to do all we can to ensure that we always have a government that allows us to seek and serve Him freely.

2. The Yearning to *Have*

The socialist ideology maintains that everyone will have equal material and financial resources, which theoretically is supposed to satisfy the individual's need for significance and importance. Yet, as we mentioned previously, in socialism, there is no such thing as private property—the government owns all sources of production and distribution. And when the government owns everything, people are unable to experience a healthy sense of accomplishment or achievement.

However, as Christians, we know that our sense of worthiness and our feeling of being deeply loved can only come through a relationship with Jesus Christ—who cares for us so much, "He Himself bore our sins in His body on the cross, so that we might die to sin and live to righteousness; for by His wounds you were healed" (1 Peter 2:24). As we seek God and fulfill the purposes for which He formed us, we experience the profound significance and satisfaction that cannot come in any other way. No political system can ever give us the fulfillment that our heavenly Father can. Even so, we should never accept any government that would try to take His place.

3. The Longing to *Do*

One tenet of socialism is that citizens join together in the goal of working for the common good—each person is a worthwhile cog in the wheel of society. This is supposed to fulfill an individual's desire for competency and security. However, as we've already discussed, there is no sense of accomplishment because there is no reward for working hard or being innovative. When socialism guides a nation, it ceases to be a land of opportunity. The system destroys the person's capacity and motivation to achieve.

Why? Because when the government tells you what you're allowed to do, where you can go, and with whom you can associate, your sense of confidence and autonomy is severely diminished.

Again, as believers we realize that these are benefits of a personal relationship with Jesus Christ. We are sealed with the Holy Spirit, who is our secure guarantee of salvation and the One who enables us in all we do (see 1 Corinthians 12:6–11 and Ephesians 4:30). As Christians, we have much to be thankful for—no matter what government we live under.

THE WEALTH OF AN INDIVIDUAL LIFE

I believe the Founders understood all of this, which is why they wrote these stirring and powerful words in the Declaration of Independence: "We hold these truths to be self-evident, that all men are created equal, that they are endowed by their Creator with certain unalienable Rights, that among these are Life, Liberty and the pursuit of Happiness."

> What we have pursued as a nation for more than two hundred years is liberty for the individual to become who he or she was created by the Father to be.

What we have pursued as a nation for more than two hundred years is liberty for the individual to become who he or she was created by the Father to be. That is why it was so important for them to ensure we were free from tyranny, bondage, and overtaxation. Let us look at this a little more closely.

1. We Are All Equal Before God

As believers, we all have access to and are responsible for obeying the Lord. The ground is level at the foot of the cross. This means the Father can appoint any of us to lead—we are not bound by artificial restrictions created by society. In many other nations, one has to be born into a ruling family to achieve prominence; however, any of us can become a statesman in the United States.

2. The Father Has Given Every Person Life

Each of us has been formed for God's purpose, and we are free to pursue His plan. It is not the government's right or responsibility to tell us how to live or what goals to achieve—that belongs to the Lord.

3. The Right to Liberty Originates with God Himself

We should never think that our emancipation has been granted by another person or government. It is bestowed upon us by Jesus—by His death on the cross through which He provided our salvation. Because of this, we cannot view the freedoms of worshiping, assembling with others, and voicing our informed opinions lightly. No person has permission to restrict the liberties that the Lord Himself has given us.

> No person has permission to restrict the liberties that the Lord Himself has given us.

A signatory of both the Declaration of Independence and the U.S. Constitution, statesman Benjamin Franklin, noted, "A nation of well informed men who have been taught to know and prize the rights which God has given them cannot be enslaved. It is in the region of ignorance that tyranny begins."

4. Finally, We Are Guaranteed the Freedom to Pursue Happiness—Not Demand It

We have the right to seek the dreams and goals that gladden our hearts. Happiness, per se, is not guaranteed by the Constitution. But the *pursuit* of it is an integral part of our national identity. In essence, the Declaration of Independence says that each person has the God-given freedom to choose the relationships, occupation, and recreation that give him or her a feeling of fulfillment, satisfaction, meaning, and purpose.

PROGRESS IN A NATION

What a privilege we enjoy as Americans! We can overcome the circumstances surrounding our birth. We are not restricted to a socioeconomic class or predetermined level of society. We can be better and achieve more than our forefathers. And we are free to serve the Lord and obey Him.

I was not born into a wealthy or important household. I wasn't even born in a noteworthy city like Washington, D.C., or New York. People usually don't even know where Dry Fork, Virginia, is. I didn't have the privileges of affluence or prominence that sometime accompany earthly success. On the contrary, Mother and I lived in one small room as I was growing up, and we didn't have much—almost nothing, really, but we got by. I had only two pairs of bib overalls—I would wear one pair as Mother washed the other.

I've never tried to make money or have a big church. I've never attempted to be someone important. I've just wanted to be obedient to God. I'm simply His servant, with a desire to walk in the center of His will. And He has blessed me with the awesome privilege of preaching the gospel all over the world every day!

Likewise, no matter where you began your life, you and your children can be as educated and wealthy as your talents, abilities, and aspirations allow you to be. Yes, that may mean putting in long and arduous hours to get ahead. You are not guaranteed an easy time or simple decisions. But as an American you are—for the most part—free to do as you will, which makes your situation unique. There are many other countries where this simply isn't true.

I fully believe the United States of America became great for three reasons: (1) its emphasis on personal freedom; (2) the understanding that if one is diligent, hardworking, conscientious, persistent, and creative, that person can improve his or her life; and (3) the fact that when people are enriching their individual lives, the nation benefits as well.

With these principles in mind, let us look at three vital attributes that are integral to economic success.

1. Purpose

What makes a person want to get up in the morning, go to work, and put in his or her maximum effort all day long? A sense of purpose and accomplishment.

Not long ago, I heard of an Australian man who visited America to investigate some state-of-the-art technology he needed for his company. He was the immediate supervisor of seven hundred people in his firm. He said, "We do blue-collar work, but every day, I try to give my employees the message that they are doing jobs that matter. Individually, they are doing important tasks and creating quality products. As a result of their labor, the company is achieving crucial objectives for our nation. That motivates them to succeed."

The truth is that everyone wants the opportunity to accomplish great things, the challenge to reach significant goals, and the encouragement of knowing what they are doing is significant and meaningful. We all need to know that what we do makes a difference.

2. Creativity

What makes any job more fun and exciting? When people are free to discover new ways of doing their tasks or of being innovative in how they approach their duties.

As you may know, one of my personal goals is to get the gospel to as many people around the world as possible, as quickly, clearly, and irresistibly as possible, through the power of the Holy Spirit, to the glory of God. That has resulted in creative new uses of the Internet and broadcasting, the translation of programs into more than one hundred languages, and constant research into emerging technologies for communicating the good news of salvation.

I get up every morning determined to seek God's will for the ministry and to see if there is anything we can do to accomplish our goals more efficiently, effectively, and with greater excellence. The Father often speaks and improves what we do through the resourcefulness and ingenuity of my coworkers and staff.

The drive to do things better always entails creativity—a fresh way of thinking about challenges or an innovative manner to motivate and encourage others to join in the task. I've found that everyone benefits when people are permitted to express their creative talent. After all, every person has the capacity to be imaginative and inventive because we are all made in the image of God—the Creator of all that exists. And when individuals are encouraged to put into practice the awesome things the Lord is doing in and through them, they approach their work with the undeniable commitment, energy, and enthusiasm that always make things better.

3. Perseverance

What makes a person pick herself up when she has been knocked down, when she has failed, or when things have simply gone awry? It is a combination of ambition and resiliency; she continues to believe that somewhere down the line, and perhaps just beyond the current horizon, things can and will be better.

I've seen it repeatedly. Individuals, companies, and nations that keep moving forward regardless of obstacles and setbacks eventually succeed. They don't pass on their troubles to others or give up. Rather, they assess the situation, figure out what must be done, and set themselves to complete the needed tasks.

James 1:12 affirms, "Blessed is a man who perseveres under trial;

for once he has been approved, he will receive the crown of life which the Lord has promised to those who love Him."

A FOCUS ON THE INDIVIDUAL INSPIRES RESPECT AND COMPASSION FOR OTHERS

Everyone wants to earn good pay, be recognized for work well done, and merit higher degrees of influence in their organization. There is absolutely nothing ungodly about this. The pathway to success is paved with a sense of purpose, creativity, and perseverance based on faith and trust in God. The individual and his or her family benefit, and so does the country where they live.

Of course, some may be concerned that a focus on the individual indicates a disregard for others. Must we abandon those who are in genuine need? Absolutely not! The opposite is true. The very point of this discussion is to show that while socialism stifles our ability to serve others, our representative republic actually sets us free to do so.

Our fourth commander-in-chief, President James Madison, affirmed: "It is the mutual duty of all to practice Christian forbearance, love, and charity toward each other." Because our own personhood is valued and protected, we have the responsibility to treat others with dignity and respect.

> While socialism stifles our ability to serve others, our representative republic actually sets us free to do so.

For example, I know a couple who work very hard because they have a handicapped child. Due to the difficulties they have experienced throughout the years, they have developed a great deal of compassion for other families with physically and mentally challenged children and strive to minister to them. They enjoy the liberty of caring for their own family and reciprocate by helping others.

Likewise, I am acquainted with a woman who is highly motivated to earn as much as she can so she can fund research into a cure for the disease that took the life of her older sister. She understands the pain this illness can cause and actively seeks to provide relief to others.

I also know a man who has relatives in an impoverished area of another nation. He devotes a large part of his earnings to provide for their physical and educational needs. Because of the opportunities that the United States has given to him and the resources he has been able to earn, he is able to help loved ones who are not so fortunate.

I am also privileged to be friends with a couple who were unable to go to college themselves but who have paid for the university educations of their children, as well as twenty-two other young people who needed assistance. They also look forward to aiding other students in pursuing their dreams through a scholarship fund they've established.

These fine men and women are very generous. They are loving, caring, self-sacrificing individuals who do not want to see anyone suffer. However, they also oppose attempts by the government to tell them how much they can spend on the charitable causes that add so much meaning to their lives. They pay taxes and obey the law— rendering "to Caesar the things that are Caesar's" (Mark 12:17)— but also reserve the right to minister in the way the Lord calls them.

ABOUT TWO BURDENS

We are to help our neighbors in need and to carry the burdens of others. But let us be clear on what Scripture teaches about these matters.

As we discussed in the previous chapter, we are called to minister to those whom the Lord puts in our paths and in our circles of influence. We do so in order to help them in ways that are not solely material. In addition to offering material help when appropriate, we impart wisdom, pray for them, show them God's love, and, above all, communicate the gospel of Jesus Christ to them.

However, we must use wisdom and discernment—seeking the Lord's guidance about when and what is appropriate assistance. There are times when our aid to another actually counteracts what the Father is trying to teach or accomplish in his or her life. We understand this more clearly when we study two words in the New Testament that are translated in English as *burden*.

1. Each One Carries His Own Load

While the Bible teaches us we are to care for those around us, not every problem is ours to solve. One of the New Testament words that is translated as *burden* is found in the book of Galatians.

The apostle Paul mentioned the first term—*phortion*—when he wrote "Each one must examine his own work, and then he will have reason for boasting in regard to himself alone, and not in regard to another. For *each one will bear his own load*" (Galatians 6:4–5). (Italics added for emphasis.) The word *load* signifies the freight that a ship normally carries or the obligations Christ has laid on us to bear. In other words, Paul charged the Galatians to take *personal responsibility* for the tasks the Lord had given them.

To attempt to help another person in *every* way—to accept all of their duties as your own—is actually an injustice. You enable their codependency and undermine their ability to care for themselves in the future.

My father died when I was only nine months old, and for most of my childhood, my mother raised me alone. Times were tough—some exceedingly so. We were very poor. For years, my mother worked at the local textile mill and brought home just $9.10 per week. That had to cover all of our needs—food, clothing, rent, and everything else. There were many times I thought, *It just isn't going to be enough.* But she would say, "We are going to trust God, and He will provide.

He has always been good to us, and He will be faithful no matter what."

You know, through those difficult seasons, we never thought that other people should shoulder our burdens. Mother and I carried our own load.

> **The Father takes full responsibility for our needs as long as we obey Him.**

And because of that, we learned in an awesome way that the Father takes full responsibility for our needs as long as we obey Him.

2. Bear One Another's Burdens

The other word for *burden*—*baros*—is also found in the writings of the apostle Paul to the Galatians. He wrote, *"Bear one another's burdens,* and thereby fulfill the law of Christ" (Galatians 6:2). (Italics added for emphasis.) This term refers to a very large and heavy load—like a boulder that has been put on a person's back or is blocking his path. Sometimes these burdens are the result of a crisis of some sort—such as an accident, the loss of a spouse, a layoff, a natural catastrophe, or a severe injury—and help is required immediately. Other times, people's burdens continue over a longer period of time. Either way, God gives us the privilege to provide assistance to a neighbor in need.

When we are called to serve, we must represent the Lord faithfully. We may offer material, physical, emotional, or spiritual support, and we may enlist others to lend a hand as well. In fact, there will be some difficulties that may require the response of the entire community or church family—such as floods, tornadoes, and hurricanes, during which people lose everything they have. In such instances, we always do well to show the love of God to those who are hurting.

Paul concludes this section in Galatians 6 by saying, "Let us not lose heart in doing good, for in due time we will reap if we do not grow weary. So then, while we have opportunity, let us do good to all people, and especially to those who are of the household of the faith" (verses 9–10). In fact, if the Father calls us to give sacrificially to another and we fail to obey Him, we are guilty of wrongdoing. James 4:17 confirms, "One who knows the right thing to do and does not do it, to him it is sin."

THE BEST WE CAN BE AND DO

God's Word is clear: "Do nothing from selfishness or empty conceit, but with humility of mind regard one another as more important than yourselves; do not merely look out for your own personal interests, but also for the interests of others" (Philippians 2:3–4). Every person we meet—whether homeless or the president of a Fortune 500 company—needs Jesus Christ as his or her Savior, and each believer has been given natural and spiritual gifts to use in the Lord's service. We may not understand what God has in store for the people we meet, but we must realize that He loves them as much as He loves us and has awesome plans for them.

> "One who knows the right thing to do and does not do it, to him it is sin."—James 4:17

We may be tempted to look at others and imagine there are limitations on what they can do or achieve, but we must always realize that the Father doesn't see as we do (see 1 Samuel 16:7). Remember, before Joseph became second in command to Pharaoh in Egypt, he was a slave and served time in jail (see Genesis 37–45). No one could have seen all the Lord had purposed for him to accomplish. Likewise, the greatest earthly monarch of Israel, King David, began as a humble shepherd (see 1 Samuel 16:11–13). And the Messiah's first cradle was a lowly manger (see Luke 2:4–20).

Count on it, looks can be deceiving. We don't have God's wisdom into people's situations and circumstances, and we may not understand His purposes, but we do know we can trust Him completely.

" 'For I know the plans that I have for you,' declares the LORD, 'plans for welfare and not for calamity to give you a future and a hope. Then you will call upon Me and come and pray to Me, and I will listen to you. You will seek Me and find Me when you search for Me with all your heart. I will be found by you,' declares the LORD, 'and I will restore your fortunes'" (Jeremiah 29:11–14).

We must realize that the people who need our assistance today may be the very disciples God uses to bless the world tomorrow.

So let's not tolerate any government that would take away our opportunity to minister to others or that would hinder people from becoming all that the Father created them to be. Because no matter what its proponents may promise, it cannot hold a candle to all that God has planned for those who love and obey Him.

> The people who need our assistance today may be the very disciples God uses to bless the world tomorrow.

Lord, give us a desire for excellence, according to
Your definition. Help us to be and do
our best. Spare us from the bondage of socialism,
and renew in us a desire to help those in need.
Show us, Father, how to grow in our relationships with You,
and how we can lead others to You.
Increase the wisdom, strength,
and love of believers throughout our nation,
Lord God, so we can pursue all the goals
You have set before us. Amen.

HOW YOU CAN HELP TURN THE TIDE

1. Dr. Stanley says, *"Scientific research studies show that people are often much less productive, efficient, creative, and concerned about the quality of the goods and services when they are under the oppression of a socialist government."*

Why do you think that a socialist government makes people less productive, efficient, creative, and concerned about the quality of their work? In what specific ways might it affect you and the lives of those around you? Do you see any evidence that socialism is increasingly prevalent in our current government? If so, how does it affect our nation and what can *you* do about it?

2. *"Individuals, companies, and nations that keep moving forward regardless of obstacles and setbacks eventually succeed. They don't pass on their troubles to others or give up. Rather, they assess the situation, figure out what must be done, and set themselves to complete the needed tasks."*

Have you ever been in a situation where you had serious troubles? Were you able to implement Dr. Stanley's principles: (1) assess the situation; (2) figure out what needed to be done; (3) and set about completing the needed tasks? Think about how you did that; and if you didn't follow those steps, plan how you could do so next time. Then, consider how these principles might be taught to others in difficult situations.

3. *"While socialism stifles our ability to serve others, our representative republic actually sets us free to do so."*

What does Dr. Stanley mean by the above statement? How might you live this out?

CHAPTER 6

THE ERODING BANKS OF PERSONAL FREEDOM

We Must Reinforce Our First Amendment Rights

In the early 1960s, I had the opportunity to preach at a Baptist church in Moscow. The Communists maintained tight control of the society, but for whatever reasons, this church was one of the few that had been allowed to stay open.

That did not mean the gospel could be preached openly, however. On the contrary, the pastor told me I needed to be extremely careful about what I said because the *Komitet Gosudarstvennoy Bezopasnosti* (better known to us as the KGB or the Committee for State Security) had informants monitoring every service.

The pastor also let me know that if I communicated something that could potentially incite the government's reproach, he would not translate it into Russian. Therefore, if I noticed that he remained silent after I had completed a sentence, I should just go on to my next point. Sadly, there were several awkward and quiet moments during that sermon.

In a government system that did not allow freedom of speech, I personally found it very difficult to preach about allegiance to Jesus Christ as our Savior and Lord and how He reconciles us with the

Father. Yes, the Communists had allowed the doors of the sanctuary to remain open, but what good was that if the gospel could not be taught there? And how could any believer ever feel at peace in a system that threatens their lives and families whenever they attempt to be obedient to Christ's mandate to lead others to salvation?

As I wondered about this, I was suddenly struck by the awful thought that this could very easily happen in our own country if we fail to remain vigilant. After all, the same stifling ideologies have been assailing our shores for more than a century. What would happen if American Christians were no longer able to tell others about Jesus or live out their faith?

This is why I am compelled to warn you and others about the restrictions the government could place upon the citizens of our nation. Whenever anyone attempts to control where we worship or what we say, be alarmed. The tide is rising.

THE HISTORICAL STRUGGLE AGAINST RELIGION

In truth, I believe Americans will face a terrible struggle to keep their religious freedom in the days ahead—a struggle that should alarm not only Christians but every citizen—regardless of their faith. Why? The reason is, whenever a nation loses its religious liberty, all other personal rights are also in danger of being lost.

> Once freedom to worship is denied, the ability to express one's opinions is also squelched.

History proves this to be true. Once freedom to worship is denied, the ability to express one's opinions is also squelched.

Those of us who remember the rise of communist governments in the first half of the twentieth century will recall how quickly Communists shut down churches and synagogues, refusing to allow those who believed in God to meet for instruction and worship services.

In fact, Russia had been known as one of the most religious countries in the world. But from the October 1917 Bolshevik Revolution forward, a policy of state scientific atheism—or *gosateizm*—was enforced. The discrimination began with the persecution of the Russian Orthodox Church because of its influence, but it quickly spread to other forms of religious faith. Those who protested were shuttled off to the forced prison labor camps known as gulags, or worse, executed. Thousands of priests, ministers, and confessors were killed due to the Communists' desire to create a worker's utopia free from God.

Of course, you may be thinking that socialism is not communism. And that is true. As we said, the *Concise Encyclopedia of Economics* defines *socialism* as "a centrally planned economy in which the government controls all means of production." Economically, communism is very similar to socialism—it likewise practices the state control of all manufacturing and distribution, although it places less emphasis on an individual's ability to produce and more on his or her needs. However, the main difference between the two is that communism has a political component. Whereas socialism generally gains power through legislative channels, communism is often dependent upon military force—sometimes requiring a violent revolution such as was seen in Russia in 1917.

This does not mean that socialism is friendly toward religious groups. Although some socialist governments are more permissive of faith, history shows that they can be just as belligerent. One only has to recall the actions of the abuses of the National Socialist German Workers' Party—otherwise known as the Nazis—who attempted to exterminate the Jews and other faiths during the Holocaust. Many tend to forget that Hitler's poisonous ideology was based on the tenets of socialism—confused by his military buildup and lack of emphasis on the social good.

> Socialism is based on government control, not public welfare. Do not be confused by what this system promises and what it actually is.

However, socialism is based on government control, not public welfare. Do not be confused by what this system promises and what it actually is.

We can see socialism's opposition to religion in the Constitution of the People's Socialist Republic of Albania, which was approved in 1976. Albania, the first nation to outlaw religion, has a constitution that declares, "The state recognizes no religion whatever and supports atheist propaganda for the purpose of inculcating the scientific materialist world outlook in people" (Article 37). People who were caught expressing their religious faith—even in their own homes— were in danger of imprisonment.

Thankfully, it did not last.

THE IMPORTANCE OF RELIGIOUS FREEDOM

Why were these societies so opposed to the expression of faith? Because a relationship with God is transcendent. He frees people from their bondage and addictions and empowers them to become more than they ever dreamed they could be. The Bible educates us, giving us the anticipation of a better life. Romans 15:4 affirms, "Whatever was written in earlier times was written for our instruction, so that through perseverance and the encouragement of the Scriptures we might have hope."

In other words, those with strong beliefs are difficult to subjugate, indoctrinate, and control. In fact, Karl Marx, the father of these socialist and communist ideologies, wrote about his opposition to Christianity, explaining, "The democratic concept holds that . . . each man is a sovereign being. This is the illusion, dream, and postulate of Christianity."

Thomas Jefferson cautioned, "Can the liberties of a nation be sure when we remove their only firm basis; that is, a conviction in the minds of the people that these liberties are the gift of God, and that they are not to be violated except by God's wrath?"

I believe that this is why the First Amendment to the U.S. Constitution—the first provision of our Bill of Rights—calls for three crucial, undeniable personal liberties: the freedoms of

- religion

- speech

- assembly

Our Founding Fathers saw these as incontrovertible gifts from the Lord. They realized that a firm belief in God—and the understanding that He created each and every man, woman, and child—is the foundation upon which all of our other rights are established.

> "These liberties are the gift of God."—Thomas Jefferson

John Adams affirmed, "You have rights antecedent to all earthly governments: rights that cannot be repealed or restrained by human laws; rights derived from the Great Legislator of the universe."

The Lord is the Creator and Sustainer of our rights as Americans, a fact we must keep in the forefront of our understanding of civics and in our public discourse. Why? Because the moment government officials convince citizens of this nation that they have the power to *grant* our liberties, they also gain the ability to *repeal* them—authority that the Founders never intended lawmakers to have.

The apostle Paul wrote, "It was for freedom that Christ set us free; therefore keep standing firm and do not be subject again to a yoke of slavery" (Galatians 5:1). As believers we must observe his admonition and refuse religious constraints that Scripture does not impose. As Americans, we can apply this warning to defend against tyranny.

I assure you, unless we act quickly and decisively to counteract the decline of this country, our children and grandchildren will not enjoy the lifestyle we have become accustomed to. We must not allow our freedoms to be eroded by misguided public servants or our ability to preach the Good News of salvation to be curtailed by any government.

A TELLTALE SIGN OF TROUBLE

One of the obvious symptoms of our nation's distress is the widespread confusion that seems to characterize the political debate. The apostle Paul assured us, "God is not a God of confusion but of peace" (1 Corinthians 14:33). Peace in this verse does not refer to an absence of war, but rather of the harmony that arises from reconciliation to the Father and from godly relationships with others. As we saw in chapter 5, once we understand our position before the Lord and His love for all humanity in providing salvation, then many of the other issues that often divide us fade. Instead of confusion, He gives us clarity as to what is right and what we should do.

So how have we gotten in so much trouble? It is because many in our country have rejected the fact that there is absolute truth, and that the Father is the source of it (see John 16:13–14). Whenever the climate of the land becomes chaotic and bewildering, you can be certain that we have drifted away from the Lord.

Whenever the climate of the land becomes chaotic and bewildering, you can be certain that we have drifted away from the Lord.

The prophet Isaiah explained: "Those who guide this people are leading them astray; and those who are guided by them are brought to confusion" (Isaiah 9:16).

Our government leaders have spun their policies and twisted the truth so radically that the electorate no longer understands what is wrong, why things have deteriorated, and what it is we should do to

correct our course. There is no consensus among the lawmakers—
they argue and squabble and never come to any clear solutions. The
country is broken, we are in danger, and something absolutely must
be done about it.

CHANGE OF FOOLS

Unfortunately, it seems that many of our leaders are focused on
change simply for the sake of doing something different. This is
rarely productive and is most often destructive. They take the attitude, "Try *something*—try *anything*. Things cannot possibly get
worse than they are now." What a devastating lack of judgment and
foresight. When no one knows where to aim, there is no way we can
hit the mark. As happens far too often, we dive into spending and
government activity—ending further from our goal than we were
before.

Repeatedly throughout Scripture and history, we have seen that
the positive transformation of a country can only come about when
godly citizens and public servants seek the Lord and obey His plans.
James 1:5 promises, "If any of you lacks wisdom, let him ask of God,
who gives to all generously and without reproach, and it will be given
to him." The Father desires for us to know His will and demonstrate
the commitment and courage to walk in it. He never leads His people
astray.

If there has ever been a time that we need God's wisdom, it is
now. I believe that those who govern our nation must ask, "Where
does the *Lord* want us to head as a nation? What does *He* want us to
do?" When He sets our goals and we agree to pursue them, amazing
things can be accomplished.

STAND UP FOR FREEDOM, OR LOSE IT

Remember, freedom of speech was included in the Bill of Rights so that people would be at liberty to voice their values and ideals. It was rooted in the understanding of right and wrong, and was designed to foster debate.

We have both the privilege and the responsibility as believers to bring clarity to the public discourse, reminding people of the truth.

But how do we do so? Jesus taught us, "Be shrewd as serpents and innocent as doves" (Matthew 10:16). We are to be perceptive and wise—realizing that those who oppose God have very clever tactics that can confuse and disarm us. We must understand their strategies and how to counteract them, while still being representatives of His love and grace.

We are to encourage morality and be examples in our society by living in truth and purity, protecting the innocence of others, especially children. We must make the choice to pursue what is right, good, and life producing—saying a loud "no" to what is wrong.

If we do not stand up now, we may lose the capacity to do so in the future. Winston Churchill warned:

> *If you will not fight for right when you can easily win without blood shed; if you will not fight when your victory is sure and not too costly; you may come to the moment when you will have to fight with all the odds against you and only a precarious chance of survival. There may even be a worse case. You may have to fight when there is no hope of victory, because it is better to perish than to live as slaves.*

God has given us our freedoms. Let us not forfeit these gifts of His grace. Instead, let us pursue them fully as we have the ability and so bless the generations that come after us.

In the next few chapters, we'll discuss how to do so.

Help us, Lord, to place renewed value on
our rights to freedom of religion, speech, and association.
Show us ways to exercise these privileges and reinforce
them so the next generation of Americans
may truly experience and protect them as well.
Amen.

HOW *YOU* CAN HELP TURN THE TIDE

1. Dr. Stanley issues a strong warning: *"In truth, I believe Americans will face a terrible struggle to keep their religious freedom in the days ahead—a struggle that should alarm not only Christians but every citizen—regardless of their faith."*

In keeping with Dr. Stanley's teaching that our proactive efforts must be done in a Christ-like manner, what can *you* do in your sphere of influence to help turn this dangerous tide?

2. *"The moment that government officials convince citizens of this nation that it has the power to grant our liberties, they also gain the ability to repeal them—authority that the Founders never intended lawmakers to have."*

Will you dedicate yourself to fall on your knees and pray for our country, then get up to take appropriate action? What actions might you take?

3. *James 1:5 promises, "If any of you lacks wisdom, let him ask of God, who gives to all generously and without reproach, and it will be given to him."*

These are serious times that require much wisdom. While you're on your knees, beg the Father for wisdom and believe He will give it to you. After you pray and give the Lord time to lead you, make a plan for what you can do to help turn the tide.

PART 2

STAND UP AND SPEAK OUT

CHAPTER 7

REFUSE TO TOLERATE THE FLOOD OF IMMORALITY

The Responsibility of "We the People"

James Garfield, the man who would become the twentieth president of the United States, gave this warning to the American people in 1877—more than a hundred and thirty years ago:

> Now more than ever before, the people are responsible for the character of their Congress. If that body be ignorant, reckless and corrupt, it is because the people tolerate ignorance, recklessness and corruption. If it be intelligent, brave and pure, it is because the people demand these high qualities to represent them in the national legislature.

What an indictment! However, as you've no doubt noticed, it is true. Our nation is a moral mess—and it is our own fault. We are responsible for the character of our political leaders. With pornography, prostitution, drug and alcohol addictions, broken families, abortion, and crime running rampant, no one can claim that our country is emotionally or spiritually healthy—and there is no legislation that can reverse all of these trends. We are a nation that is far from clean and pleasing before God.

The good news is that, in general, the American people say they want greater morality in their culture—to abolish abortion; reduce the prevalence of crime; pornography, and prostitution; and lower the rate of divorces and addictions. The change, however, will only take place when people take a real, meaningful stand for morality.

BEGIN WITH OUR OWN MINDS

The truth is, most Americans *say* they do not want trash in their lives. They don't want litter on their yards or garbage on their television sets. I have never met a parent who wanted his or her child to watch or engage in anything immoral. And I have never met a married person who wants his or her spouse to be involved with pornography or to be sexually promiscuous.

Unfortunately, people often have higher standards for those they love than they do for themselves. What they wouldn't allow another to view or participate in, they themselves do without a second thought; and it affects their thought processes and decision-making skills in terrible ways they probably do not realize.

This is because our minds are working all the time—taking in every message and image the world wishes to feed us. The goal of these messages is to program our thinking so that we embrace what the lifestyle advertisers, opinion-makers, and politicians are selling: messages that are often contrary to what God has called us to. As believers, we cannot realistically expect the lost to combat these messages and to live godly lives. Scripture tells us that those without Christ operate according to the flesh—in their naturalness (see 1 Corinthians 2:12–14). They don't think about spiritual things; nor can we expect them to function by them because they simply cannot do so. They only way to combat ungodliness is by the weapons of faith in God and reliance on the Holy Spirit, which they don't have. Jude 1:10 explains, "These men revile the things which they do not understand; and the things which they know by instinct . . . by these things they are destroyed."

This is why it is up to us, as Christians who have the internal witness of the Spirit, to lead the way and be examples of godliness and morality to our lost and dying world. We must help others to not destroy themselves.

Regrettably, Christians—including our children and teens—watch as much ungodly content as non-believers. Even more devastating, according to one highly reputable survey firm, rentals of pornographic movies at hotels actually increase anytime there is a Christian convention in town.

> It is up to us, as Christians who have the internal witness of the Spirit, to lead the way and be examples of godliness and morality to our lost and dying world.

As people called to represent our Savior, the Lord Jesus, in holiness, why would we do this? Why would we allow such destructive materials to influence our minds? We are the ones responsible for stopping the rising tide of immorality in our culture, but we will never have any credibility among the citizens of our nation as long as we are engaged in the same things they are.

People sometimes ask me where I draw the line in watching movies and programs. A friend of mine told me once that she only watches motion pictures that she would feel comfortable showing to her seven-year-old niece and nine-year-old nephew. That sounds like a pretty good policy to me. The movies I watch demonstrate positive moral values—loyalty, honesty, and the triumph of good over evil. And usually, they have already been screened and recommended by people who know my movie tastes and standards.

Some may think this is very limited or that I am too straight-laced, but Proverbs 4:23 commands, "Watch over your heart with all diligence, for from it flow the springs of life." If we don't pay attention to what influences us, we will face all kinds of difficulties. This is because the things we meditate on become part of who we are;

they affect everything—our relationships, jobs, even how we view our citizenship.

TAKE THESE TWO STEPS *NOW*

So how do we combat the rising tide of immorality? First and foremost, we pray. Then, we speak up.

1. Pray

In order to combat the surging increase of immorality, Christians need to pray that the Father will move in the hearts and lives of those who are lost and living ungodly lifestyles, including the ungodliness that may be in their own lives.

I strongly encourage you to become part of or to start a prayer group that meets regularly. Intercede for one another, your families, friends, coworkers, neighborhoods, city and state governments, national leaders, churches, and businesses. Pray for our country to return to an open acknowledgment of the Lord and to the principles of His Word.

2. Speak Up

After we pray and get the Lord's guidance, we need to speak up at every opportunity to reinforce the values of decency, modesty, fidelity, purity, and courtesy in our culture. Those who live in a godly manner generally do not suffer from a specter of guilt and shame hanging over them. Instead, they are almost always more joyful, free, and grateful.

In fact, the apostle Paul wrote this about people who walk in step with the Spirit: "The fruit of the Spirit is love, joy, peace, patience, kindness, goodness, faithfulness, gentleness, self-control; against such things there is no law" (Galatians 5:22–23). Note the last phrase in the verse above: "against such things there is no law."

Although we cannot lawfully require people to live in a way that is godly, we must work to prevent legislation that actively promotes ungodliness—anything that legally condones or institutionalizes ungodly behavior. Rather than tolerating and funding reckless behavior, we must encourage others to exercise self-control, with the freedom to make choices regarding their own spending, health, and responsibilities.

The template provided by Paul gives us a wonderful checklist as we make decisions. For each choice we ask:

- Does it demonstrate godly love?

- Does it produce joy?

- Does it promote peace?

- Does it originate from patience?

- Does it give birth to kindness?

- Does it show God's goodness?

- Does it foster faithfulness?

- Does it inspire gentleness?

- Does it motivate us and others to self-control?

We must respond to what is wrong by voicing what is right and edifying. There is tremendous benefit in giving people a positive alternative.

For example, think of specific difficulties and problems challenging your family, friends, work, and community. What do you perceive would be the correct remedy or most appropriate course of action? Examine your beliefs. Are they upright and honorable? Think about the benefits you receive from obeying God and how it helps others when you act in an admirable manner. Then pray and search Scripture, asking the Lord to reveal to you if what you're practicing is truly in line with His will. When He shows you what to do, explain to those involved why it might be the best course of action for them as well.

Those who obey the Father are in the best possible position for receiving and enjoying all of His many blessings. On the other hand, those who rebel against God are setting themselves up for terrible consequences. They may benefit temporarily, but ultimately they will regret their choices.

> **Those who obey the Father are in the best possible position for receiving and enjoying all of His many blessings.**

TAKE A STAND

So what are the things we must stand against? In Ephesians 4:17–24, the apostle Paul instructs the following:

Affirm together with the Lord, that you walk no longer just as the Gentiles also walk, in the futility of their mind, being darkened in their understanding, excluded from the life of God because of the ignorance that is in them, because of the hardness of their heart; and they, having become callous, *have given themselves over to* sensuality *for the practice of every kind of impurity with* greediness. *But you did not learn Christ in this way, if indeed you have heard Him and have been taught in Him, just as truth is in Jesus, that, in reference to your former manner of life, you lay aside the old self, which is being corrupted in accordance with the lusts of deceit, and that you be renewed in the spirit of your mind, and put on the new self, which in the likeness of God has been created in righteousness and holiness of the truth. (Roman added for emphasis.)*

As we discussed, we cannot expect the lost to act in a godly manner because they do not have the internal witness of the Holy Spirit to show them what the Lord wants them to do. Paul confirmed this, reiterating that those without Christ continue to be "darkened in their understanding" (Ephesians 4:18). He also said that they have become callous, sensually impure, and greedy—giving us a guideline for what they seek and what we must defend against.

These characteristics strike at the very core of what we said were the three basic aspirations that reside in the heart of every man and woman:

- the desire to *be*—feeling acceptance and belonging

- the yearning to *have*—achieving a sense of worth and love

- the longing to *do*—attaining an understanding of one's own competency and security

How do the characteristics manage to strike at the core? They are

- callous—no longer sensitive to the sanctity of human life and no longer seeing people as being created and loved by God

- sensually impure—given over to every form of sexual immorality out of their need to possess, yet instead of fulfilling their need for a sense of worth, the actions debase it further, destroying any idea of how to actually achieve it

- and greedy—succumbing to the allure and false security of wealth (they compare themselves to others and base their security and competency on what is fleeting—therefore never truly attaining it).

As believers, we are to comprehend why these attitudes struggle to prevail in our hearts, and do all we can to stand against them—both in our own lives and in our nation. We cannot fight them out of anger or outrage over the actions of the lost, who, we must realize, truly do not know any better. Instead, we do so out of compassion for the lost, knowing that they could find everything they seek in an intimate, personal relationship with Jesus Christ.

Let's now take a closer look at callousness, sensual impurity, and greed:

1. Callousness: Indifference Toward Life

The first thing we must consider is that our Supreme Court sits in a chamber whose doors are engraved with a representation of the Ten Commandments—the sixth of which proclaims, "You shall not murder" (Exodus 20:13). Yet its members passed a ruling that allowed for the legal execution of unborn children. How could this be? How is it possible that members of our chief judicial body demonstrated such little regard for the sanctity of human life? Why did they ignore Scripture, which says, "Do not kill the innocent or the righteous" (Exodus 23:6–8)?

They did it either because they lacked knowledge of the spiritual reality or because they blatantly denied what they knew to be true. Of course, some simply do not acknowledge that it is the Lord who gives life to each and every person—the unborn, the elderly, and the disabled. Only He can cause the sperm and egg cells to unite in a way that produces life. Acts 17:24–27 teaches:

> *The God who made the world and all things in it, since He is Lord of heaven and earth, does not dwell in temples made with hands; nor is He served by human hands, as though He needed anything, since He Himself gives to all people life and breath and all things;*

and He made from one man every nation of mankind to live on all the face of the earth, having determined their appointed times and the boundaries of their habitation, that they would seek God, if perhaps they might grope for Him and find Him, though He is not far from each one of us.

The Father is the author and finisher of all that exists—and He is the One who gives each soul significance, purpose, and vivacity. He has allowed each of us to be born in our unique circumstances and times, with our distinctive skills, talents, and yes, even our limitations, for a purpose. We must never lose sight of that truth.

Psalm 139:13–16 reminds us:

You formed my inward parts;
You wove me in my mother's womb.
I will give thanks to You, for I am fearfully and wonderfully
  made;
Wonderful are Your works,
And my soul knows it very well.
My frame was not hidden from You,
When I was made in secret,
And skillfully wrought in the depths of the earth;
Your eyes have seen my unformed substance;
And in Your book were all written
The days that were ordained for me,
When as yet there was not one of them.

This Scripture communicates a message to each and every person: you are important, loved, and significant in God's eyes. He cares for you, no matter what you may have done in your life or who you are. You are precious to Him—and He wants you to know Him.

Many people either do not realize this or do not believe it. Perhaps

> You are important, loved, and significant in God's eyes.

they've been wounded and made to feel worthless. Or maybe they felt the need to protect themselves and became centered on their own desires in the process. Regardless of the cause, they developed a low view of others.

Think about what abortion and euthanasia communicate to our children. Not all people are desirable or acceptable? Not everyone has value? There are people who should not be permitted to live?

Does that thinking extend to those who become sick? To those who can no longer work or contribute to society? To those who are too old or too handicapped to experience what society defines as a "quality" life?

Every person is imperfect to some degree. Yet we are all loved by the Father. He has purposes that He has created each of us specifically to fulfill—and that includes working through what the world perceives as our faults and limitations (Ephesians 2:10).

2. Sexual Immorality: The Pain and Shame

Much of our confusion about the worth of the individual is a direct result of our society's permissiveness toward sexual relations outside of marriage. It is a dangerous cycle: with callousness toward life comes the devaluation of one's body. And with increased immorality comes progressive desensitization about the worth of human life.

Of course, there may be some reading this who are wondering, *Why would the Lord prevent us from participating in activities that seem so normal and natural? After all, isn't sex a gift God's given to us to enjoy freely?* In fact, there may even be some Christians who have not given themselves to Jesus fully because they want to be free to do as they please. They don't like the idea that there is a God in heaven who would prevent them from experiencing the gratification they desire.

Friend, do not be caught in the trap of sexual sin, because it is absolutely devastating. This is why 1 Corinthians 6:18 admonishes, "Flee immorality. Every other sin that a man commits is outside the body, but the immoral man sins against his own body." You hurt yourself immeasurably when you engage in sexual sin.

Its power is in its deceptive offer for immediate pleasure without penalty, but there are terrible consequences associated with it. At first people may not realize the harm they are doing. They may think they are just having fun, but the wounds it inflicts on the human soul are terrible.

As people participate in immoral acts, they feel shame and dishonor—experiencing increased separation from the Lord and further isolation from the care and acceptance they really want. Their consciences set off alarms that what they are doing is wrong, but they ignore the warnings, shutting themselves off from communication from the Holy Spirit. Trying to soothe their sense of detachment from the Father, the addiction to sexual sins grows because they want to feel like they truly belong and are worthy of love—even if it's only for a moment.

Chaotic feelings of shame and confusion rise up within them. They try to hide their pain from others, which means they are forced to lie to their loved ones about their bondage, damaging their closest, most important relationships. Isolated from godly influences and under the control of sexual sin, the deep emptiness within them escalates; and their resistance to temptation fails. Soon enough, they are willfully engaged in disobedience to God. They sink deeper into an empty, wretched life that makes them feel as if they are nothing.

Sexual immorality can destroy people quickly and make them feel utterly hopeless. They get to the point where they feel so degraded that they don't think the Father could ever love them again. So they deny Him before He can reject them.

Trust and obey God's boundaries. The truth of the matter is, God calls us to live pure lives because He wants us to enjoy all the blessings He has for us. He puts boundaries on sex—commanding that it be between a man and a woman who are married to each other—because He cares about what happens to us physically. He does not do so to be cruel or unfair. He does it because He loves us and wants us to experience life at its very fullest. He gives us His commands for our benefit—to prevent us from destroying ourselves.

However, no matter what sin you've committed or what sexual addiction has trapped you, the Father is *not* your enemy. On the contrary, He is your Defender, desiring to free you from whatever bondage you find yourself in.

> The Father is *not* your enemy. On the contrary, He is your Defender, desiring to free you from whatever bondage you find yourself in.

This is why He teaches us in Romans 6:13–14, "Do not go on presenting the members of your body to sin as instruments of unrighteousness; but present yourselves to God as those alive from the dead, and your members as instruments of righteousness to God. For sin shall not be master over you."

Through Christ's gift on the cross and His power over sin, we have the ability to choose what has control over us—either the urges of our fleshly nature or the Holy Spirit. How do we make that choice?

- *First, we must acknowledge whatever we have done that is contrary to God's Word.* First Thessalonians 4:3–4 tells us, "This is the will of God, your sanctification; that is, that you abstain from sexual immorality; that each of you know how to possess his own vessel in sanctification and honor." We should agree with the Lord about whatever sin we've committed and ask Him to show us how to live in a manner pleasing to Him.

- *Second, we must be genuine in our repentance.* The Father will not accept our confessions if we're still playing the blame game or are merely sorry we were caught. We must be honest and sincere in our admission of guilt. We must also be willing for God to change the direction of our lives.

- *Third, we must understand the source of our actions and take responsibility for them.* What triggered our sin? Was it fear or insecurity? Was it a need for intimacy, acceptance, or fulfillment? Was it a lack of self-esteem, a drive to conquer, or a desire to "get even" for some wrong done to us? Whatever the root of our actions, we must understand it so we can stand firm against temptations when they assail us.

- *Finally, we should ask God to help us forgive ourselves.* Going through life believing we are failures sets us up to fall again. We must open our hearts to the Father so He can teach us how to live in godliness—as vessels for His use that can lead others to salvation.

The reality is that God created us to be loved and to demonstrate love to others. This is why His awesome forgiveness is always available to all who are willing to recognize they need Him and accept His provision. The Father's desire is that we would experience the hope, care, and fellowship with Him we were formed to enjoy.

A few years ago, I received a letter from a woman that absolutely made me weep. She grew up in a home where she was constantly assailed by her parents' violent tempers, emotional abuse, sexual exploitation, alcohol addiction—you name it. By the time she was a teenager, she was on drugs and felt as if she was an absolute nobody. She did not think anyone cared for her or that her life was worth living. Even when she called the churches in her area, the pastors refused to speak to her. She finally decided to be a prostitute so she could finance her drug problem and dull the pain she felt in her heart. As I read her letter, I realized that a soul simply doesn't feel any lower than she felt. Rejected, abused, full of shame, and devoid of hope, she got in her car and began to drive.

Although it seemed as if no one on earth was willing to help this girl, there was One in heaven who was working to reach her and get her attention. After four days in her car without drugs, she flipped on the radio and heard an In Touch program. It was a simple interview where I said something about Jesus' forgiveness being available to the hurting soul, no matter what's happened in his or her life.

In her letter, she wrote that right then, she pulled her car over, stopped on the side of the road, and accepted Jesus Christ as her Lord and Savior. She declared that in that moment, the Father set her free of her addictions and hopelessness.

Understand, this is not a Charles Stanley or an In Touch Ministries story. This is a testimony of God's awesome love for us. He is the One who engineered everything necessary to reach that girl. He is the One who knew exactly what she needed to hear—at exactly the moment she needed to hear it.

The truth is, every person is born with an inclination toward some type of sin—and that desire isn't completely erased from us at the time we accept Jesus as our Savior. It is a part of our fallen human nature, and our challenge in life is to trust God to empower us to resist the temptations that come across our paths and to fulfill our need for love and acceptance.

Glorify God with our bodies. Of course, as we lead others into a growing relationship with Jesus and call our fellow Christians to live godly lives, they may feel somewhat ashamed or embarrassed because of the things they have done; they may even lash out because of it. They may doubt that there is true freedom from the pain and shame of their sexual immorality and may mock the hope you offer.

However, the fact that they feel guilt is positive evidence that the Holy Spirit is still powerfully at work in their lives. We cannot give up on them. We must reach out to them and continue loving them in the hope they will accept the forgiveness of their sins and renew an intimate relationship with God, which is what they truly long to experience.

We must also make sure we remain pleasing and honorable to the Lord—being worthy representatives for the sake of His name. It's dangerous to think we can ever let down our guard against sin. First Peter 5:8 clearly tells us, "Be on the alert. Your adversary, the devil, prowls around like a roaring lion, seeking someone to devour." We must remain diligent and observant at all times in order to refrain from yielding to his lures.

Think about it: the world sometimes sees believers as hypocrites because of those who do not practice what they preach. Instead of relying on God and being examples of the purity they speak about, "believers" may point the finger at others. The stories are heartbreaking—teachers who rail against homosexuality but are later found to be addicted to pornography; those who preach family values but are discovered to be in adulterous relationships. The damage they do cannot be overstated.

If we wish to be a true light to our nation and stem this tide of immorality, we must make sure we keep a clear conscience before God. This is why Paul taught,

The body is not for immorality, but for the Lord, and the Lord is for the body. Now God has not only raised the Lord, but will also raise us up through His power. Do you not know that your bodies are members of Christ? Shall I then take away the members of Christ and make them members of a prostitute? May it never be! Or do you not know that the one who joins himself to a prostitute is one body with her? For He says, "THE TWO SHALL BECOME ONE FLESH." But the one who joins himself to the Lord is one spirit with Him. Flee immorality. Every other sin that a man commits is outside the body, but the immoral man sins against his own body. Or do you not know that your body is a temple of the Holy Spirit who is in you, whom you have from God, and that you are not your own? For you have been bought with a price: therefore glorify God in your body. (1 Corinthians 6:13–20)

The apostle Paul put the burden on us as believers—we must act in a godly manner. We must live as temples of the Holy Spirit—fleeing immorality and glorifying God in our bodies. When we are fully engaged in doing what is *right* before the Father, there is little time or energy left for getting bogged down in all the arguments and debates about what is wrong in His eyes.

Our responsibility is to hold out the true hope of heaven, the love of God, and the opportunity for a cleansed, free, productive, purposeful life in Christ, this is what the lost will respond to and what will ultimately divert them from the path of sin. It is the future the Father has envisioned for His children—a life worth pursuing, no matter what a person's past may have been.

3. Greed: God or Mammon?

We've discussed the problems of being callous toward life and of sexual immorality. When people no longer value the life God has given or their own being, they have to find worth somewhere, and they usually turn to possessions.

Therefore, the final trend we must combat is *greed*, the temptation to succumb to the false security of wealth.

> "Do not weary yourself to gain wealth . . . [f]or wealth certainly makes itself wings."
> —Proverbs 23:4–5

People long to feel competent and safe, yet they will never do so as long as they build their lives on something as illusory and temporary as money. Proverbs 23:4–5 warns, "Do not weary yourself to gain wealth, cease from your consideration of it. When you set your eyes on it, it is gone. For wealth certainly makes itself wings like an eagle that flies toward the heavens."

So many of our nation's citizens pursue affluence at the cost of everything else—their communities, friendships, families, and even their own health and well-being. Some do so by becoming workaholics while others do so by illicit means.

And what do they buy? More things that do not satisfy the long-ings within them. They may purchase items that indicate worth in an outward fashion—such as cars, homes, jewelry, beauty treatments, or what have you. Or they may acquire things that attempt to dull their inner pain—such as alcohol and drugs. Sadly, this only drives them further from what they really need.

What a waste of life and resources. Can you imagine what awe-some things might be done if people were to redirect all that effort and energy into pursuing the kingdom of God? Think about the change that could occur in our nation if the money that was spent on things that harm us physically, psychologically, relationally, and spiri-tually were instead spent on godly programs and resources that edify humanity—teaching people how to have a fulfilling relationship with the Lord. Undoubtedly, we would be absolutely amazed.

We could reach those who have never heard the gospel, comfort those who are hurting, and give hope to those who have none.

Those who are hungry could be fed, and people who are cold could be clothed and sheltered.

The uneducated could learn to read and write, and those who are unskilled could become proficient in the abilities they need to earn a living and improve their quality of life.

We would not have to look to our government to help others—because *we* could do it ourselves. And it would all be done in the name of the One who saves our souls from the grave.

This is why Jesus taught:

Do not store up for yourselves treasures on earth, where moth and rust destroy, and where thieves break in and steal. But store up for yourselves treasures in heaven, where neither moth nor rust destroys, and where thieves do not break in or steal; for where your treasure is, there your heart will be also. . . . No one can serve two masters; for either he will hate the one and love the other, or he will be devoted to one and despise the other. You cannot serve God and wealth. For this reason I say to you, do not be worried about your life. (Matthew 6:19–21, 24–25).

Our Savior wants us to invest our resources and energy in eternal things that will last—not in temporary things that will lead us further from Him. In a practical sense, this means we . . .

- provide for the work of the gospel both locally and around the world through our tithes and offerings.

- are examples of His faithfulness to others—giving generously and providing food and clothing to those in need.

- honor God no matter what it costs us—trusting Him to provide for all our needs as we obey Him.

A CHALLENGE TO THE CHURCH

The truth of the matter is that it's time our churches have serious discussions about the sanctity of life, the need for abstinence, and the godly use of our resources. We need to educate our children and teens about the danger of materialism, the importance of purity, and the great damage sexual immorality can cause to people's bodies, minds, emotions, and relationships. We must instruct them about the significance of every life—regardless of age or limitations—and the importance of remaining in the center of God's will for our lives so we can be His vibrant witnesses here on earth.

Additionally, we must reach out. Countless men and women in our nation are saddled with tremendous guilt over things they've done that have harmed themselves and others. We must lovingly call them to

> **We cannot change their pasts, but we can show them the possibilities of a future with the Savior.**

confession and repentance—showing them God's mercy and demonstrating the hope that comes with His forgiveness. We cannot change their pasts, but we can show them the possibilities of a future with the Savior. They should not be shunned, ridiculed, or subjected to gossip. Instead, they should be encouraged to pursue a life of devotion to God.

THEIR CRIES MATTER TO GOD

Perhaps as you've traveled through the years, you have noticed signs advertising something called "Happy Hour." And perhaps, like I have, you've observed the great irony in that term. I've spoken to people who have frequented them, and they assure me they have never found any true joy there. In fact, those pastimes just served to amplify the disillusionment and disappointment the participants felt.

In many ways, I see our nation as seeking their own Happy Hour. People in our society seem to want a place of escape—where their sins are hidden in the dark and where they can find relief for their pain. However, as believers, we know that they will never find solace as long as their transgressions lay buried in their hearts, unacknowledged and unforgiven. The lost and hurting are everywhere—needing the love and acceptance Christ offers.

Jesus said, "It is not those who are healthy who need a physician, but those who are sick. But go and learn what this means: 'I DESIRE COMPASSION, AND NOT SACRIFICE,' for I did not come to call the righteous, but sinners" (Matthew 9:12–13). And as His representatives, we are to reach out:

- to the elderly man who has been abandoned in the nursing home.

- to the mother who fears for the safety of her children.

- to the abused child—crying because of his pain and confusion.

- to the gambler who has lost everything—even his identity.

- to the prostitute in her feeling of worthlessness.

- to the homosexual suffering from AIDS.

- to the alcoholic bearing the devastating effects of his addiction.

- to the drug addict who sees no hope in his future.

- to the person caught in pornography full of regret and shame.

- to the woman who has had an abortion, in her loss and guilt.

- to those who are reaping the consequences of the bad decisions they've sown and those who suffer because of the selfish choices of others.

- to whomever is lost and needs to know what it means to be loved, accepted, worthy, competent, and secure in God's forgiveness and grace.

These are the people whom Jesus reached out to, and we need to reach out as well. Society may discard them, forget them, and even judge them, but our Savior loves them, and He wants them to return to Him.

THE NATION WE DESERVE

President James Garfield was right—we *do* have the nation we deserve. Because if we continue to refuse to reach out to our fellow Americans with the gospel, and if we deny our own responsibility to obey the Lord, nothing will ever change.

But if we will cleanse our hearts, obey God regardless of the consequences, and reach out to the lost, the Father can transform our country in ways we could never imagine.

As I've said before, the choice is ours.

Will we be found faithful?

What will you do to reach the lost in your community?

Forgive us, Lord, for allowing rampant immorality
to engulf us as a nation. Help us put an end to
the unrighteousness in our land—
starting with our own hearts and minds. Purify us and
refine us as Your people, that we might reflect
Your glory and lead others to You. Amen.

WHAT *YOU* CAN DO TO
HELP TURN THE TIDE

1. *"We are the ones responsible for stopping the rising tide of immorality in our culture, but we will never have any credibility among the citizens of our nation as long as we are engaged in the same things they are."*

In the statement above, Dr. Stanley is referring to ungodly activities (such as pornography or sexual impurity) that Christians engage in to the discredit of Christianity. Honestly examine your own heart and life. What activities or attitudes do you allow yourself to participate in that not only break the heart of God but also taint your witness to unbelievers? Believe that the Father has the power to change your heart and repent wholeheartedly before Him.

2. *"Although we cannot lawfully require people to live in a way that is godly, we must work to prevent legislation that actively promotes ungodliness—anything that legally condones or institutionalizes ungodly behavior."*

Take note of two very important messages above from Dr. Stanley: we *can't* legislate morality but we *can* work to prevent legislation that actively promotes ungodliness. You, as a citizen of this great country, have a vote and a voice. Give prayerful thought to how you can use both to turn the tide.

3. Dr. Stanley admonishes us not to be angry or outraged *"over the actions of the lost, who, we must realize, truly do not know any better. Instead, we [speak out against sin] out of compassion for*

the lost, knowing that they could find everything they seek in an intimate, personal relationship with Jesus Christ."

Carefully consider your attitude and feelings toward those whom you disagree with politically or whose lives are in a spiritual mess. In your stand for what is right, are you compassionate and heartbroken by their brokenness, or are you angry? Know that love has the power to turn the tide, whereas anger only adds to its force of destruction.

CHAPTER 8

BOLDLY HOLD OUR LEADERS ACCOUNTABLE

The Time Has Come for Greater Accountability

"We the people" have a great deal of responsibility for the rising tide of pain and suffering in our country, but there's plenty that must be shouldered by our leaders as well. And it is our duty to hold them accountable.

Many people assume that God's Word deals only with individual spirituality and that it has nothing to say about politics or about the leadership of a nation. However, read the following verses and you will see the Lord is very interested in the way our officials rule:

- "Without wise leadership, a nation is in trouble, but with good counselors there is safety" (Proverbs 11:14 TLB).

- "If a king is kind, honest and fair, his kingdom stands secure" (Proverbs 20:28 TLB).

- "When you remove corrupt men from the king's court, his reign will be just and fair" (Proverbs 25:5 TLB).

- "With good men in authority the people rejoice; but with the wicked in power, they groan" (Proverbs 29:2 TLB).

- "A just king gives stability to his nation, but one who demands bribes destroys it" (Proverbs 29:4 TLB).

These warnings are for us, and they are just as accurate and powerful today as they were the day they were written. When the leaders of a country are unrighteous—in rebellion against God—the people face misery. But when the officials love and honor the Lord and are in right standing with Him, the people rejoice.

KNOW THAT LEADERSHIP IS ALWAYS "UNDER GOD"

As we discussed in chapter 2, it is God who appoints people to govern nations. The ability to lead is a privilege people receive due to either His *permissive* or *purposeful* will.

The Father's *permissive* will means that He *allows* something to happen—sometimes in response to ungodliness. He lets the consequences of people's bad decisions run their course in an effort to bring them to repentance. An excellent example of this is the Babylonian captivity. First Chronicles 9:1 confirms, "Judah was carried away into exile to Babylon for their unfaithfulness."

On the other hand, God's *purposeful* will is His plan for mankind that cannot be changed or thwarted, such as His plan to bring Judah back from Babylon and resettle the people in the land of their inheritance. "Thus says the LORD, 'When seventy years have been completed for Babylon, I will visit you and fulfill My good word to you, to bring you back to this place" (Jeremiah 29:10). Just as He promised, when the seventy years were completed, the people returned.

Understanding this, we see why it is important for those in leadership to acknowledge the Father's will, plans, and commands, He holds their lives and their countries in His hand (see Psalm 103:19). Godly leaders—monarchs, presidents, and lawmakers—can make a huge difference in how quickly their people return to the Lord and get back on track in obedience to Him.

This was the case when the Lord was about to send His judgment to the Ninevites. Jonah 3:6–10 reports,

> *When the word reached the king of Nineveh, he arose from his throne, laid aside his robe from him, covered himself with sackcloth and sat on the ashes. He issued a proclamation and it said, "In Nineveh by the decree of the king and his nobles: Do not let man, beast, herd, or flock taste a thing. Do not let them eat or drink water. But both man and beast must be covered with sackcloth; and let men call on God earnestly that each may turn from his wicked way and from the violence which is in his hands. Who knows, God may turn and relent and withdraw His burning anger so that we will not perish." When God saw their deeds, that they turned from their wicked way, then God relented concerning the calamity which He had declared He would bring upon them. And He did not do it.*

Because this ruler decided to honor the Lord, his people were saved from certain disaster.

Godly Leaders

King David understood that godly leadership was crucial to the success of the nation of Israel. With his last words, he explained:

> *The Spirit of the LORD spoke by me,*
> *And His word was on my tongue.*
> *The God of Israel said,*
> *The Rock of Israel spoke to me,*

"He who rules over men righteously,
Who rules in the fear of God,
Is as the light of the morning when the sun rises,
A morning without clouds,
When the tender grass springs out of the earth,
Through sunshine after rain."
Truly is not my house so with God?
For He has made an everlasting covenant with me,
Ordered in all things, and secured;
For all my salvation and all my desire,
Will He not indeed make it grow?
But the worthless, every one of them will be thrust away like
    thorns,
Because they cannot be taken in hand;
But the man who touches them
Must be armed with iron and the shaft of a spear,
And they will be completely burned with fire in their place."
    (2 Samuel 23:2–7)

Notice several key words and phrases in this passage:

1. *God is the Rock of Israel.* He knew that the foundation on which the nation—and the very earth—had been established was the goodness and faithfulness of the Lord (see Deuteronomy 4:33–35; Psalm 22:28).

2. *Righteous kings rule in the fear of God.* Leaders should stand in awe of the Father, knowing that He is ultimately in charge of all things. They should also understand that the ability to rule is a profound responsibility to those who are blessed with it (Psalm 33:16–22).

3. *Righteous rulers are like the sunshine after a rain.* In other words, righteous rulers create the conditions for their land to succeed and prosper. Because of the Lord's wisdom and sovereignty, godly leaders are able to keep their nations orderly, secure, and flourishing as they obey Him. It is God who causes growth, but He uses good rulers to establish conditions that foster it (see 1 Chronicles 22:11–13).

4. Worthless leaders do not submit to God's hand. Because they do not submit to God, David says, they will be thrust away like thorns. Thorns throughout Scripture are a symbol of trouble and trial; they are useless plants that are gathered in heaps and burned. David notes that rulers who refuse to seek the Lord do not survive. Although they are difficult to deal with and remove, their end is sure (see Psalm 9:4–6; Proverbs 16:12).

> It is God who causes growth, but He uses good rulers to establish conditions that foster it.

God Raises and Removes Leaders

As we discussed, leaders must have it firmly in their minds and hearts that God is the One who gave them the office they hold. He raised them up, and He can remove them as well. They must heed the words of Psalm 2:10–12, "O kings, show discernment; take warning, O judges of the earth. Worship the LORD with reverence and rejoice with trembling. Do homage to the Son, that He not become angry, and you perish in the way, for His wrath may soon be kindled. How blessed are all who take refuge in Him!"

Leaders must understand that if they become arrogant, God will act against them, rebuking them, and admonishing the people they govern. They do not have the right to act as they please—seeking their own wealth, goals, or greatness. Rather, they are accountable to the Lord God in all they do. Ultimately, all of us will be judged by the Father, and He will test the quality of each man's work (see 1 Corinthians 3:11–15). Psalm 75:1–7 explains:

> *We give thanks to You, O God, we give thanks,*
> *For Your name is near;*
> *Men declare Your wondrous works.*

"When I select an appointed time,
It is I who judge with equity.
The earth and all who dwell in it melt;
It is I who have firmly set its pillars. . . .
I said to the boastful, 'Do not boast,'
And to the wicked, 'Do not lift up the horn;
Do not lift up your horn on high,
Do not speak with insolent pride.'"
For not from the east, nor from the west,
Nor from the desert comes exaltation;
But God is the Judge;
He puts down one and exalts another.

Leadership within Boundaries

The authority of leaders in our country is curtailed, not only by our U.S. Constitution but also by the Word of God. It is clear that the role of government is to preserve order, restrain evil, and promote justice. Government has a threefold responsibility to safeguard us, which includes:

- *Militarily defending* us from both foreign and domestic entities that would attempt to weaken, control, invade, or destroy us.

- *Protecting* us from faulty infrastructure—such as dangerous highways and bridges—that connects intra- and interstate travel.

- *Shielding* us from those who would steal from us or destroy our economy.

The government, as established by our Founding Fathers, is not answerable for our basic needs or responsible for the choices we as individual citizens make in our lives. Rather, its duty is to protect our interests so that we can work hard, earn an honest living, and make progress in the pursuit of our personal goals. Our duty is to provide for our own needs and to bear our own burdens.

Outside the Boundaries

Of course, our officials have the right to enforce existing laws concerning public order and safety. But what are some of the things that the United States government does *not* have the Constitutional authority to do?

- It is not authorized to dictate matters related to personal health. Our legislators do not have legal or constitutional permission to control our medical decisions—what physicians we see, which medications we take, or what procedures we have done.

- It also cannot determine our dietary choices—what we eat, drink, or feed ourselves, our children, and our families.

- It cannot tell us where we can or cannot live, or what type of residence we must choose. The government does not have authority to tell us how big or small our houses should be, or how we must furnish them.

- Our legislators cannot limit or define who our friends and associates are. Likewise, they cannot tell us which groups or churches to attend or join.

- The government cannot control where, how long, or for whom we work, nor how we spend our after-tax money; it cannot dictate what kind of vehicles we drive or determine how much energy we are allowed to purchase or consume.

- The legislatures also cannot tell us how to raise our children or provide for their educations.

You may be smiling as you read this list, thinking, *These privileges are central to our rights as citizens. Our lawmakers wouldn't try to touch them.*

However, allow me to point out two facts:

First, there are governments elsewhere in the world that regulate individual citizens in each of the ways I've identified above. One example of this is the Chávez regime in Venezuela. Under Hugo Chávez, companies in the steel, oil, cement, rice processing and packaging, and utilities industries have been nationalized. Private property and food has been confiscated. Political opponents have been ostracized and denied their rights. And opposition by media outlets is squelched. Sadly, there is increasing pressure to allow the laws of other nations to be established in our country.

Second, our rights do not protect themselves—they require our vigilance because there will always be people who attempt to control us through legislation. Even now, some government officials believe American citizens are not capable of making wise choices for their individual lives. They tell us we are not savvy enough to make good business decisions, not equipped to understand both sides of a debate, and not compassionate enough to care for others. They argue we need leaders to make our choices for us.

You see, it is just as James Madison warned, "Since the general civilization of mankind, I believe there are more instances of the abridgement of freedom of the people by gradual and silent encroachments by those in power than by violent and sudden usurpations."

> It is easier for tyranny to take hold slowly by convincing the populace of its need for the government's help than to infringe upon it forcefully.

He understood that it is easier for tyranny to take hold slowly by convincing the populace of its need for the government's help than to infringe upon it forcefully. The state overreaches—taking more authority in our lives and regulating our actions. This means there are more forms to fill out, more bureaucracies necessary to manage the process, and more taxes to pay for the increase in services. Eventually, we are enslaved—and the most disheartening part is that we've agreed to it. Make no mistake: our Founding Fathers never intended the government to micromanage our individual lives.

DEMAND LEADERSHIP VERSUS CONTROL

Throughout the years, I've encountered people in ministry who have tried very hard to control those who attended their churches. Rather than allowing God to transform them from within, they attempted to force their church members to conform to their standards of behavior. Regrettably, the more a pastor or minister struggled to change their church members, the more the congregation responded in hostility to them and resentfulness toward the Lord. The people eventually rebelled against the pressure. These leaders often became so frustrated at their failure to alter their people that they felt compelled to leave the ministry—dishonoring the Father and ruining their futures. How true the admonishment of Proverbs 28:16: "A leader who is a great oppressor lacks understanding."

As a pastor, it is my responsibility to seek God's guidance and communicate the vision He gives me to the congregation, directing the members of the church in an understanding, compassionate, and deliberate way. I must give people opportunities to serve others and to become all the Father has created them to be. I must also lead by example. I cannot *force* anyone to do anything.

Leadership Principles for Our Country's Lawmakers

The leadership of a democracy is not so different from the administration of a church. Our government leaders have the ability to speak to very large groups of people—either directly in a conference or rally or by media broadcast—and inspire their constituents to become the best they can be.

What should they be communicating? Let me give you three key principles:

Vision. Proverbs 29:18 tells us, "Where there is no vision, the people are unrestrained." Leaders must describe their dreams and plans for who we can be as a nation, what we might do, and how we can reach our potential. They do so in order to channel the energy and resources of the people in a positive manner. They point us toward the goal we desire to reach—the ideal we are pursuing.

Responsibility. A leader must also clarify what the responsibilities of each person and party are. I meet regularly with my teams at both the church I pastor and at In Touch Ministries, our international broadcast ministry. I keep my fellow coworkers accountable for the duties they have been assigned. And I always remind them to trust the Lord—seeking His guidance for the details and doing what is best for the people. As long as we obey God, we can leave all the consequences to Him, knowing He will care for all of our needs.

It is not the responsibility of the government to rule over the details of our lives. Rather, it reminds us of what we are accountable for and what good citizenship means.

Service. Our government officials are also in a prime position to be role models of servant leadership to those in our society.

Jesus gave us the supreme example of sacrificial service through His atoning death on the cross. But even before the crucifixion, He modeled servant leadership in extraordinary ways. The apostle John gives us one such example in this account from the Last Supper:

Jesus, knowing that the Father had given all things into His hands, and that He had come forth from God and was going back to God, got up from supper, and laid aside His garments; and taking a towel, He girded Himself. Then He poured water into the basin, and began to wash the disciples' feet and to wipe them with the towel with which He was girded. . . . So when He had washed their feet, and taken His garments and reclined at the table again, He said to them, "Do you know what I have done to you? You call Me Teacher and Lord; and you are right, for so I am. If I then, the Lord and the Teacher, washed your feet, you also ought to wash one another's feet. For I gave you an example that you also should do as I did to you." (John 13:3–5, 12–15)

Likewise, Jesus taught us, saying, "The one who is the greatest among you must become like the youngest, and the leader like the servant. For who is greater, the one who reclines at the table or the one who serves? Is it not the one who reclines at the table? But I am among you as the one who serves" (Luke 22:26–27).

The importance of servant leadership simply cannot be overstated.

When These Three Principles Are Lacking

When leaders fail to communicate vision, responsibility, and service, two problems arise:

1. It is much more difficult to trust them.

2. There is a rise in corruption.

Consequence #1: Loss of Trust. Do you have confidence in your lawmakers? Do you believe they are honorable individuals? We would like to believe that our legislators have our best interests at heart. But the truth is, we can no longer make that presumption.

Our laws are only as effective as our lawmakers are morally dependable. They must communicate the reason for the regulations and our responsibility in upholding them. They must also put those laws into practice as our example.

Unfortunately, that often isn't the case. We see greed in our government officials and in how they create legislation out of their desire for more power and money. Likewise, their lack of moral clarity is on display whenever they pass laws that condone and legalize immoral behavior.

In fact, the leaders with the poorest morals tend to be the loudest voices protesting any person or organization that advocates a godly lifestyle. The following are two tactics these leaders utilize when objecting to those who call for decency and integrity in our country:

First, they appeal to people's emotions rather than their ethical principles. They find the most sympathetic case possible and demonstrate how cruel and heartless it would be to withhold rights or services to them. This is sheer manipulation, and we must recognize it as such.

Second, they belittle anyone who opposes them—calling them any number of names and marginalizing their opinions. How can we possibly trust those on either side of the aisle who show us so little respect? We simply cannot put our confidence in those who openly disparage what we believe and the moral standards we have chosen to live by.

Consequence #2: cover-ups, confusion, and corruption. When leaders have no vision but merely tell their listeners what they wish to hear, when they avoid communicating our responsibility, and when they fail to demonstrate servant leadership, corruption cannot be far behind. There are government officials who promise the world to their constituents, but the people they really serve are those who line their pockets.

> **Words can inspire, but they can also enslave us, especially when our lawmakers do not say what they mean.**

You can see it in the way they draft their legislation. Why should any bill require hundreds of pages for implementation? Are these officials attempting to conceal the control they are taking over the people? Are they creating confusion so they can profit?

Think about the wording on measures presented at election time that are up for a simple yes-or-no vote. Some of these proposals are so convoluted in their phrasing, you may be voting in favor of something you actually oppose.

Words can inspire, but they can also enslave us, especially when our lawmakers do not say what they mean.

DEMAND ACCOUNTABILITY

More than ever, we need to hold our elected officials accountable for their words and actions. God's Word tells us:

- "Where there is no guidance the people fall, but in the abundance of counselors there is victory" (Proverbs 11:14).

- By wise guidance you will wage war, and in the abundance of counselors there is victory" (Proverbs 24:6).

- Without consultation, plans are frustrated, but with many counselors they succeed" (Proverbs 15:22).

Our nation's Founding Fathers understood the wisdom established in these verses from Proverbs. Because of this, they ensured that power was not consolidated into the hands of a king or even in one branch of government. They realized a system of checks and balances was necessary in order to guarantee that no one group of people could dictate the future of the nation. Alexander Hamilton explained:

The regular distribution of power into distinct departments; the introduction of legislative balances and checks; the institution of courts composed of judges holding their offices during good behavior; the representation of the people in the legislature by deputies of their own election. . . . They are means, and powerful means, by which the excellences of republican government may be retained and its imperfections lessened or avoided.

Our elected officials have a role to fill, but they must be reminded not to overstep their boundaries. Much of what is happening at the national level seems to involve conflict among the branches of government—a tug-of-war for power our Founding Fathers tried to avoid.

We see federal judges who attempt to legislate from the bench, interpreting law according to their own judgment, rather than by our nation's legal history and Constitution. Presidents do the same, enacting regulations through executive orders—often crossing into territory that is not theirs to influence. We also have legislators who are supposed to represent the people, but who often ignore the wishes of their constituents.

Uphold the Constitution

At times I can't help but ask, has anyone read the Constitution lately? Why are we abandoning a system that's worked extremely well for the past two hundred years?

I challenge you today: Get a copy of the Constitution and read it. Study it with your children, your loved ones, your friends, and your coworkers. Discuss it. Know the foundation of our government. Understand how things are supposed to function. Only when we do that can we hold our elected officials accountable for fulfilling their specific roles in government.

We must insist that lawmakers abide by the Constitution, and that they choose judges—both at the appellate level and in the Supreme Court—who will make decisions based on the strict rule of law. We must also be resolute in demanding that our leaders stick to U.S.

precedents rather than give in to the legal standards of other countries. Pressure by foreign governments to conform to their values is increasing, not decreasing—especially through entities such as the United Nations. Our leaders must stand firm against their demands.

Take on the Mantle of Moral Leadership

We must also insist that our leaders take on the mantle of moral leadership, such as we saw in the presidency of Abraham Lincoln. Most people respect Lincoln and regard him as a great president. Let me give you just one example of his moral and spiritual leadership.

On March 30, 1863, President Abraham Lincoln issued the following *Proclamation Appointing a National Fast Day.* As you read through this brief document, ask yourself, is this what our government leaders believe today? Most of our leaders, regardless of their political parties, admire Lincoln and say they wish to emulate him. But do they see our nation in the same light as Lincoln did?

Whereas, the Senate of the United States, devoutly recognizing the Supreme Authority and just Government of Almighty God, in all the affairs of men and of nations, has, by a resolution, requested the President to designate and set apart a day for National prayer and humiliation:

And whereas it is the duty of nations as well as of men, to own their dependence upon the overruling power of God, to confess their sins and transgressions, in humble sorrow, yet with assured hope that genuine repentance will lead to mercy and pardon; and to recognize the sublime truth, announced in the Holy Scriptures and proven by all history, that those nations only are blessed whose God is the Lord:

And, insomuch as we know that, by His divine law, nations like individuals are subjected to punishments and chastisements in this world, may we not justly fear that the awful calamity of civil war, which now desolates the land, may be but a punishment, inflicted upon us, for our presumptuous sins, to the needful end of our national reformation as a whole People? We have been the recipients of the choicest bounties of Heaven. We have been preserved, these many years, in peace and prosperity. We have grown in numbers, wealth and power, as no other nation has ever grown. But we have forgotten God. We have forgotten the gracious hand which preserved us in peace, and multiplied and enriched and strengthened us; and we have vainly imagined, in the deceitfulness of our hearts, that all these blessings were produced by some superior wisdom and virtue of our own. Intoxicated with unbroken success, we have become too self-sufficient to feel the necessity of redeeming and preserving grace, too proud to pray to the God that made us!

It behooves us then, to humble ourselves before the offended Power, to confess our national sins, and to pray for clemency and forgiveness.

Now, therefore, in compliance with the request, and fully concurring in the views of the Senate, I do, by this proclamation, designate and set apart Thursday, the 30th day of April, 1863, as a day of national humiliation, fasting and prayer. And I do hereby request all the People to abstain, on that day, from their ordinary secular pursuits, and to unite, at their several places of public worship and their respective homes, in keeping the day holy to the Lord, and devoted to the humble discharge of the religious duties proper to that solemn occasion.

All this being done, in sincerity and truth, let us then rest humbly in the hope authorized by the Divine teachings, that the united cry of the Nation will be heard on high, and answered with blessings, no less than the pardon of our national sins, and the restoration of our now divided and suffering Country, to its former happy condition of unity and peace.

What an incredible statement of humility before the Lord and proclamation of faith in His care! Would any of our national leaders be bold enough to make such a proclamation today? Sadly, I don't think so.

> "Recognize the sublime truth, announced in the Holy Scriptures and proven by all history, that those nations only are blessed whose God is the Lord."
> —Abraham Lincoln

INSIST THAT LEADERS ANSWER TO THEIR CONSTITUENTS

Too often we lose sight of the fact that those who hold office in our democratically elected government are answerable to us, the voting citizens of the nation. We have the right to demand accountability from those we elect—not only at election time but in an ongoing way.

Why? Because it is up to us to ensure that our leaders behave in a responsible manner—not only with their stewardship of our resources but also with their power to regulate our lives. You see, the more accountability we insist on, the better our lawmakers will perform. Without oversight, they simply do not do their best.

A lack of answerability generally results in the following:

- *Poor performance*: Our elected officials see no reason to work hard to fulfill their promises and responsibilities because no one will question them about their progress.

- *Division*: Our delegates are more likely to point fingers and blame others when programs fail because there are no concrete roles or responsibilities.

- *Missed opportunities*: Instead of using their resources and time to solve real problems in a timely manner and proactively prevent difficulties, lawmakers may wait until it is too late to address an issue. This generally costs a great deal more—in time, resources, and manpower.

- *Waste*: There are no personal consequences for overspending: public funds are not the legislators' money but no one asks how resources they spend are utilized. Think about it—when you don't keep an account of your money, aren't you more likely to squander it on unnecessary purchases? For example, consider these government expenditures:

  - Television advertising for the U.S. Census during the 2011 Super Bowl: $2.5 million.

  - Renovation of an apartment building set for demolition in Shreveport, Louisiana: $1.5 million.

  - Construction of an overpass for a railway crossing so that the 168 residents of a Nebraska town don't have to wait for trains as they go by: $7 million.

  - Ensuring there is sufficient poetry in our nation's zoos: $1 million.

  - Research on the impact of climate changes on wildflowers in a Colorado ghost town: $500,000.

  - Federal grant for the preservation of musical group memorabilia for the Grateful Dead: $615,000.

  - U.S. government studies of video games such as *World of Warcraft* for communication strategies: $2.9 million.

  - Medicare payments to clinics that have never treated a patient because they exist only on paper: $35 million.

  - Renovation of five seldom-used ports of entry on the U.S.–Canada border in Montana: $77 million.

- Federal grant awarded to test ways to control private home appliances in Martha's Vineyard, Massachusetts, from an off-site computer: $800,000.

Every year, literally billions of tax dollars are being spent that have absolutely nothing to do with bettering our lives or improving this nation. Truly, the need for accountability is great.

Have Empathy for Those Who Struggle

Of course, there may be people who think I just don't understand the difficulties that our fellow Americans face and the good that some lawmakers are trying to do. To those, I have a two-part response.

First, I acknowledge I had the privilege of being raised by a godly mother, which means I had an excellent influence who taught me God-honoring values from early on in my life. Not everyone has that.

However, as I mentioned previously, I grew up in what most people would consider poverty. My father died when I was a baby, and there was no Social Security in those days to help Mother as she tried to provide for us. She raised me on her own, working at local textile mills to support us. She did not ask the government for money—she simply worked as hard as she could to afford the basics of shelter, clothing, and safety.

Of course, I did my part as soon as I could by selling newspapers and doing various jobs during the summers. But it never dawned on either my mother or me to seek out government subsidies to pay for my education. Yes, a member of my church gave me some financial assistance so that I could attend college. However, I still had to be *very* frugal throughout those years. I worked long, difficult hours in a textile mill, gave a tenth of my earnings to the church, and never spent what I didn't have. Thankfully, because I was on a pay-as-I-studied basis, I didn't graduate from college or seminary with thousands of dollars of loans to repay.

So yes, I understand what it is to grow up in poverty and make very difficult sacrifices to achieve my goals. Life wasn't easy during those early years, but I believe God worked through it all to teach me about His character.

Second, I understand the troubles our fellow Americans face because there are people from every walk of life at First Baptist Atlanta. This surprises most people. However, visit the church and you will see people from a huge variety of national, cultural, racial, and socioeconomic backgrounds attending our services. We actively practice our belief that the gospel is for everyone and that God's Word teaches us to love *all* people—extending the hand of Christian fellowship, regardless of any superficial societal distinctions.

Because of this, I see the struggles my church family members must endure, and I understand how difficult life is for some of them. I see them doing their absolute best to handle their challenges in the most honorable manner possible.

Friend, they don't want more federal assistance. They want leaders who understand and respect their challenges—lawmakers who are godly, trustworthy, and moral, who will not increase their burdens.

Wake Up and Ask

This is why I feel it is time we wake up and ask, to whom are we entrusting our future? Are we electing men and women who have strong convictions? Do we really know what our government officials think? Are they voting as they said they would and enacting legislation that upholds our values? Are we holding them accountable for what they promised us?

It is time we do so, asking not only what they plan to do but also what they truly believe. It is a person's convictions that drive his or her behavior. What is truly heartbreaking is that some officials who advocate a moral lifestyle have secret lives that dishonor their public stances. If our lawmakers are immoral and untrustworthy, how can we ever hope they will pass laws that are for our good?

Instead, let us hold our leaders responsible for their actions. May we never forget the words of one of our nation's founders, William Penn: "Those people who will not be governed by God will be ruled by tyrants."

We must choose, my friend, to be led by those who are governed by God—just as we are.

———————

Father, renew in us a desire for greater accountability—
both in our own lives and from our leaders.
Speak to our lawmakers as only You can.
Convict them of their responsibility—first to You
and second to the people You have
allowed them to lead. Amen.

———————

HOW *YOU* CAN HELP TURN THE TIDE

1. *"The government . . . is not answerable for our basic needs or responsible for the choices we as individual citizens make in our lives. Rather, its duty is to protect our interests so that we can work hard, earn an honest living, and make progress in the pursuit of our personal goals."*

Dr. Stanley's statement above expresses responsibility both for our government and for ourselves. Are you meeting *your* responsibilities? How can you hold our elected officials responsible to meeting theirs?

2. James Madison warned: *"There are more instances of the abridgement of freedom of the people by gradual and silent encroachment by those in power than by violent and sudden usurpations."*

What examples do you see in your own lifetime of the kind of encroachments indicated above? While behaving as Christ would have you, what can you personally do to protest such encroachments?

3. President Abraham Lincoln wrote, *"We have been preserved, these many years, in peace and prosperity. We have grown in numbers, wealthy and power, as no other nation has ever grown. But we have forgotten God."*

How can we, today, act upon the powerful call for prayer issued by President Lincoln? In the excerpt above, what similarities do you see between 1863 America and today?

CHAPTER 9

STAND AGAINST THE STORM CLOUD OF PRIDE

Nothing Stops Progress Like Arrogance

When I was born, in 1932, the thirty-first president of the United States, Herbert Hoover, was in office. This means I've lived long enough to have experienced, at least to some degree, the work and influence of fourteen presidents. I've also watched countless men and women go to their state capitals or to Washington, D.C., with great humility, hopefulness, and reliance upon the Father to do good for their fellow Americans.

Sadly, I've seen far too many return home defeated, filled with arrogance and cynicism. It seems the power they experienced warped their perspectives—and they began to place far too much emphasis on their own personal effectiveness.

Interestingly, Alexander Hamilton also took note of this very phenomenon. He said, "A fondness for power is implanted, in most men, and it is natural to abuse it, when acquired."

How was this zeal for authority exhibited in the lives of some of our nation's leaders? In the most simple terms, they no longer admitted their need for God or their accountability to others.

STAND AGAINST PRIDE—IN OURSELVES

What I observed in these men and women is the very definition of pride, and it absolutely devastated their lives—almost beyond recognition.

Proverbs 16:18 tells us plainly, "Pride goes before destruction, and a haughty spirit before stumbling." Arrogance is extremely damaging because it is an overemphasis on an individual's personal power, abilities, and talents. People see themselves as the sole source of their own success and happiness, and their attention is focused on their self-interests.

However, before we ever consider the pride that plagues our leaders, we need to stop and take an honest look at our own hearts. Do we attribute the good things in our lives to our own power, abilities, and talents?

Or do we recognize that they come from the Father? Do we acknowledge His sovereignty in all things?

Romans 12:3 warns, "Through the grace given to me I say to everyone among you not to think more highly of himself than he ought to think; but to think so as to have sound judgment, as God has allotted to each a measure of faith." Before we consider the flaws of our leaders, we need to first examine ourselves and submit our own hearts to God (see Matthew 7:5).

Why? Because as we take note of our leaders' actions, it must not be with a harsh, prideful mind-set. Rather, it should be in humility, understanding that we do not bear the burdens they carry, nor do we realize why the Lord has allowed them to rise to their positions in government. They may face challenges, and God may have purposes that we simply don't see or comprehend. But when we begin with an attitude of humility and submission to the Father, we are more likely to see the issues at hand with His wisdom. We are also more apt to turn to Him in prayer and godly action than against our leaders in anger.

STAND AGAINST PRIDE— IN OUR LEADERS

People who are in positions of power and leadership are even more susceptible to the dangers of pride than we may realize. With the power they yield, those who are constantly lobbying for their favor, and the people who work for them who cater to their decisions, it is often difficult for them to remain unaffected.

Yet Jesus was clear, "Everyone who exalts himself will be humbled, but he who humbles himself will be exalted" (Luke 18:14). Eventually, all of us must face our weaknesses, failures, and faults.

Regrettably, most people plagued with a conceited attitude cannot admit their mistakes. To do so would undermine the entire basis for their self-worth. After all, they grow to believe they know better than everyone else. To confess their errors would be to admit they have weaknesses.

They eventually become unable to acknowledge how their behaviors contribute to the problems they're experiencing. Instead of accepting that their actions are only hurting the situation, they try harder to make their strategies work—throwing more money at a problem or creating more bureaucracy to regulate an issue.

And isn't that exactly the problem we're facing with our government officials today?

LISTEN TO THE LORD'S WARNING

Based on the testimony of Scripture and history, we can be certain God has many avenues for dealing with people in leadership—especially those who refuse to acknowledge Him. In fact, He can remove a person from power in the twinkling of an eye (see 1 Kings 22:30–37; Acts 12:21–23).

Isaiah 2:17 assures us, "The pride of man will be humbled and the loftiness of men will be abased; and the LORD alone will be exalted." This is because only the Father is in absolute control. As we noted earlier, He is omniscient (all-knowing), omnipresent (with us wherever we are, during every moment), omnipotent (all-powerful), and omni-benevolent (unconditional and perfect in His love for us). He is eternal, and He is always in charge.

Yes, there are times when He allows dishonorable and cruel people to rise to power in a country. But He often does so in order to convict His people of their ungodly ways and lead them to repentance.

Therefore, we should take note: if God allows leaders that oppress us, pass ungodly laws, or are contrary to His values to take power, it may very well be He has done so to warn us that things simply aren't right in our nation.

OVERCOME FOUR ARROGANT FALLACIES IN OUR NATIONAL THINKING

The truth is that apart from the Lord, *anything* that builds our sense of importance and safety as a country can become a stumbling block of pride—regardless of whether it's America's great wealth, military might, technological advances, generosity, or influence in the world. Any of these things can lead us to the point where we believe we don't need Him.

> Apart from the Lord, *anything* that builds our sense of importance and safety as a country can become a stumbling block of pride.

So what are some of the wrongful attitudes that have become stumbling blocks for us? What are the areas of pride we must overcome in order to return to the Father? I see four main errors in thinking that must be eliminated:

- Fallacy #1: God is not involved.

- Fallacy #2: We will inevitably survive.

- Fallacy #3: No one else is hurt by our actions.

- Fallacy #4: We must ensure that life is fair for everyone.

Let's examine these one at a time.

Fallacy #1: God Is Not Involved

The first misleading notion is one we've already identified as being at the very heart of arrogance. It is the idea that the Lord is irrelevant and does not have any part in our national discourse. At best, those who support this erroneous concept believe He exists, but that we should not mention Him out of deference to those who do not acknowledge Him (see Romans 1:21). At worst are those who deny He is real at all (see Psalm 14:1). Both are horribly wrong.

As believers, we know the very opposite is true: the Father exists and has everything to do with the spiritual health of our country. In fact, Psalm 33:12 proclaims, "Blessed is the nation whose God is the LORD." He is actively involved in every aspect of our lives and He will do what is necessary to get our attention.

One has only to look at the witness of biblical history to see that the Father's purposes are always redemptive and instructive, though sometimes His methods are beyond our understanding.

- When the world was full of wickedness, the Lord sent the great flood, saving only Noah and his family on the ark (Genesis 6–9).

- When the people of Israel needed to be freed from their devastating bondage in Egypt, God sent the ten plagues to ensure their release (Exodus 6–11).

- Throughout the Book of Judges, whenever the people forgot the Lord, He sent invading armies to convict them of their sinfulness and godly rulers to help them return to Him.

- And as we noted in chapter 8, when Judah was unfaithful to the Father, He sent the people to Babylon, allowing them to return to the land of their inheritance after seventy years of exile.

Each of these trials presented the people with an opportunity to look to heaven—to return to God and ask what He wanted them to learn.

The same is true for us. The Father is trying to get our attention, calling us to repentance and to a deeper relationship with Him. It is our responsibility to obey what He is saying to us. Hebrews 12:25–29 warns,

See to it that you do not refuse Him who is speaking. For if those who did not escape when they refused him who warned them on earth, much less will we escape who turn away from Him who warns from heaven. And His voice shook the earth then, but now He has promised, saying, "YET ONCE MORE I WILL SHAKE NOT ONLY THE EARTH, BUT ALSO THE HEAVEN." This expression, "Yet once more," denotes the removing of those things which can be shaken, as of created things, so that those things which cannot be shaken may remain. Therefore, since we receive a kingdom which cannot be shaken, let us show gratitude, by which we may offer to God an acceptable service with reverence and awe; for our God is a consuming fire.

The Lord will continue to shake this country if we refuse to listen to Him. Rather than dismiss His involvement in our national affairs, we should acknowledge His presence and submit to His awesome ways.

Fallacy #2: We Will Inevitably Survive

Of course, there may be those who think, "No matter how hard God allows our country to quake, we'll be fine. We've made it through worse. Nothing is stronger than American resolve."

This is the second great fallacy in our thinking, and I hope you see the arrogance in it. The prophet Isaiah tells us, "Behold, the nations are like a drop from a bucket, and are regarded as a speck of dust on the scales; behold, He lifts up the islands like fine dust. . . . All the nations are as nothing before Him, they are regarded by Him as less than nothing and meaningless" (Isaiah 40:15, 17).

The Lord God is transcendent; He is above and beyond all that exists. When Isaiah says the countries of the world are "as a speck of dust on the scales," it means they do not weigh anything at all to Him. He could hold all the continents of the earth in His hand and not even notice. Our minds cannot comprehend the awesome greatness, power, wisdom, and understanding of the Father.

> Our minds cannot comprehend the awesome greatness, power, wisdom, and understanding of the Father.

When we think we can withstand the wrath of God on the basis of American resolve, we are badly mistaken—and our pride will be our downfall.

The truth of the matter is that the United States has been extremely blessed by the Lord. We have an abundance of natural resources in our land and are feeding far more than our own people with the produce we harvest. However, we must never take for granted that these blessings are His provision to us. We must cherish Him for what He has freely bestowed.

The Lord warned Moses, "If you ever forget the LORD your God and go after other gods and serve them and worship them, I testify against you today that you will surely perish. Like the nations that the LORD makes to perish before you, so you shall perish; because you would not listen to the voice of the LORD your God" (Deuteronomy 8:19–20).

There was a limit to God's long-suffering with Israel, and the same is true for us. It may seem as if there are sinful practices in our nation that have continued without His detection or comment. But let me assure you, He *does* notice and the time is coming when He will make His displeasure concerning our sinfulness known.

When He does, it will not be pleasant.

Fallacy #3: No One Else Is Hurt by Our Actions

The third fallacy addresses a prevalent idea in our nation that we should be able to do whatever we please as long as we're not hurting anyone else. Many have come to believe that our personal decisions have no real impact on the rest of the country. However, the choices we make as individuals *do* impact the rest of the citizens in our land. We are accountable for our actions—not only to the Lord but also to one another.

Some who are reading this may genuinely doubt God cares about what you or anyone else does in our personal lives and in the privacy of our own homes. After all, 1 Corinthians 6:18 says, "The immoral man sins against *his own body*." (Italics added for emphasis.) If you're only injuring yourself, what does it really matter? Why should what is done between consenting adults be anyone else's business?

The truth is, however, others are *always* impacted in some way by our actions.

Our sin affects our relationships with God. The Father sees everything we do. When you and I sin, we shut Him out of important areas of our lives, which are desperately in need of His presence and healing. Our sin prevents us from experiencing the fullness of a relationship with Him and all the wonderful things He has planned for our lives.

What we do always affects our attitudes, beliefs, and actions—and that most definitely impacts others. Nothing we do remains private forever.

Luke 6:45 tells us, "The evil man out of the evil treasure brings forth what is evil; for his mouth speaks from that which fills his heart." In other words, whatever we focus our attention on will—in due course—be expressed through our lives.

The process of sin is the same for everyone, whether a person is serving in an official governmental position or not. The progression begins with a thought, ultimately affecting our imaginations and then becoming uncontrollable desires. Finally, we consent; we give in to our fleshly longings. After a time, our transgressions become habits—actions we cannot control, no matter how we try.

The apostle Paul expressed the terrible power of sin: "I am of flesh, sold into bondage to sin. For what I am doing, I do not understand; for I am not practicing what I would like to do, but I am doing the very thing I hate" (Romans 7:14–15).

Eventually, these deeds harm our characters, manifesting themselves in observable behavior such as bitterness, irritability, isolation, and abusive speech. We hurt not only ourselves but also our loved ones and all the people who could have been saved through our testimonies.

What began in private becomes part of who we are in public—and we may not even realize it has happened. In a sense, this is why the next fallacy in our national thinking is so dangerous. When people do not realize they are being ruled by sin, they also do not realize their transgressions are affecting their ability to make wise choices.

Fallacy #4: We Must Ensure that Life Is Fair for Everyone

The fourth misconception is that the government can ensure everyone has identical access to opportunities, with the standards of equality decided by those in authority, such as legislators and judges. This is an arrogant assumption. What human being—or nation—is adequately equipped to resolve what is just and fair for everyone? Inevitably, their opinions will be formed on the basis of their own experiences and understandings.

Their conclusions will also be subject to the sins that control them.

For example, some people may say that because we have freedom of speech and everyone should be permitted expression, it is only fair that pornographers be allowed to have their say. Because of their own proclivities and backgrounds, they may be blind to the destructive nature of such illicit materials.

However, I wonder if those same individuals would agree that based on fairness and free speech a person has the right to publish classified information that potentially puts their own loved ones in danger. They most likely would say—and rightly so—that this falls outside the boundaries of freedom of speech. Their personal interest in the content transmitted—namely intelligence that impacts the safety of their loved ones—affects their decision. In other words, they would make a judgment relative to their situation and values.

Such a subjective standard is a poor foundation for a country. There are as many opinions about fairness as there are people in our land. This is why the laws of our society must be based on God's holy and unwavering Word, which does not vary according to a person's age, ethnicity, culture, education, or socioeconomic background (see Psalm 89:14–16; Proverbs 1:2–7; 16:11). His commands are universal and applicable to all people. Psalm 111:6–8 assures us, "The works of His hands are truth and justice; all His precepts are sure. They are upheld forever and ever; they are performed in truth and uprightness."

This does not mean I think our desire for fairness is wrong. On the contrary, I believe the Father put the understanding of right and wrong and the longing for justice within us to reveal Himself to us (Romans 1:20–32). However, when we stray from His absolute standard, we face serious consequences.

> **The Father put the understanding of right and wrong and the longing for justice within us to reveal Himself to us.**

Why People Are Averse to Living by God's Laws

Why are some people so opposed to living their lives according to God's standards? Why do they see His gracious commandments as only punitive and limiting? I believe there are two reasons.

1. Many are ruled by their fleshly nature. The apostle Paul clarified the inherent issue when he wrote, "Those who are according to the flesh set their minds on the things of the flesh . . . because the mind set on the flesh is hostile toward God; for it does not subject itself to the law of God, for *it is not even able to do so*" (Romans 8:5, 7; italics added for emphasis). They don't want to do things the Lord's way because they do not comprehend the value of what He teaches us. This means that as believers, we have a responsibility to teach them about the efficacy of the Father's commands.

2. People are drawn to the immediate pleasure that sin promises. People are seeking to alleviate the pain, loneliness, or unworthiness they feel. This is why temptations are so powerful—they offer the gratification of a person's longings for acceptance and significance without penalty. However, we know there are consequences to sinful behavior.

James 1:14–15 explains, "Each one is tempted when he is carried away and enticed by his own lust. Then when lust has conceived, it gives birth to sin; and when sin is accomplished, it brings forth death." People are seeking fulfillment, but are finding only deeper disappointment (see Proverbs 16:25).

TURN BACK TO GOD

The truth of the matter is that the more we give in to our pride and attempt to operate outside of God's commands, the greater our troubles.

Founding Father and governor of Virginia Patrick Henry said it best: "It is when a people forget God that tyrants forge their chains. A vitiated state of morals, a corrupted public conscience, is incompatible with freedom. No free government, or the blessings of liberty, can be preserved to any people but by a firm adherence to justice, moderation, temperance, frugality, and virtue; and by a frequent recurrence to fundamental principles."

So what can we do to turn away from our pride and back to God? What does He require from us to restore and heal a nation? The Father shows us the way through His words to King Solomon:

> *The LORD appeared to Solomon at night and said to him, "I have heard your prayer and have chosen this place for Myself as a house of sacrifice. If I shut up the heavens so that there is no rain, or if I command the locust to devour the land, or if I send pestilence among My people, and My people who are called by My name humble themselves and pray and seek My face and turn from their wicked ways, then I will hear from heaven, will forgive their sin and will heal their land." (2 Chronicles 7:12–14)*

As Creator of all that exists, God has every method at His disposal to help us return to Him and restore our country. Psalm 103:19 affirms, "The LORD has established His throne in the heavens, and His sovereignty rules over all." He can do anything He pleases—adjusting the activity of the weather, creatures, and even nations to suit His purposes and save His people from the difficulties that assail us.

> God has every method at His disposal to help us return to Him and restore our country.

What We and Our Nation Must Do

The Father gives us four directives that are necessary for our return to Him:

1. God requires our hearts to be right. If those who govern us insist on their own plans and purposes, He will permit them, and us, to face the consequences of their actions. But if our country is to return to Him—cleansing our hearts of all our self-sufficiency and sinfulness, and agreeing that His path is the very best for our lives—He will forgive and heal our land.

2. The Father tells us to pray. God calls our nation to humble ourselves before Him and cry out for His mercy, forgiveness, and guidance. For our country to change, we must submit the control to Him—committing ourselves to His wisdom and obeying His commands.

3. The Father tells us to seek Him. The Lord is always looking for those who will sincerely surrender themselves to Him, giving Him full authority in their lives. This can be done only when we genuinely know and trust Him. Therefore, we must pursue an intimate relationship with Him—daily knowing His holy character in more profound ways. We must also pay attention to what He is focused on and learn to see the world from His perspective.

4. God tells us to turn from our wicked ways. This means we must change our attitudes and behavior—choosing to do what is right. We must make the decision to live according to His Word, knowing that obedience to Him always brings blessing, no matter how difficult it is.

Throughout these steps, the Father teaches us how to be free from the tentacles of pride and how to practice humility. As Proverbs 29:23 teaches, "A man's pride will bring him low, but a humble spirit will obtain honor."

What God Will Do

What does the Lord promise to do in response to our obedience to Him? He says, "I will hear from heaven, will forgive their sin and will heal their land" (2 Chronicles 7:14).

1. He will hear from heaven. Understand what an awesome privilege it is to have the ear of God Almighty! Whenever the people of Israel cried out to the Father, He always released them from their bondage—whether it was from Egypt, Babylon, or other oppressors.

Whenever you feel as if our national situation is hopeless, remember this principle: the Father hears your cries for mercy, forgiveness, and rescue (Psalm 40:1–4). Nehemiah testifies, "When they cried to You in the time of their distress, You heard from heaven, and according to Your great compassion You gave them deliverers who delivered them from the hand of their oppressors" (Nehemiah 9:27).

2. He will forgive our sin. Only our Savior has the right and authority to pardon our sins because He paid the penalty for them. Look at the awesome promises He gives us in His Word to do so:

- "You, Lord, are good, and ready to forgive, and abundant in lovingkindness to all who call upon You" (Psalm 86:5).

- "As far as the east is from the west, so far has He removed our transgressions from us" (Psalm 103:12).

- "Who is a God like You, who pardons iniquity and passes over the rebellious act of the remnant of His possession? He does not retain His anger forever, because He delights in unchanging love. He will again have compassion on us; He will tread our iniquities under foot. Yes, You will cast all their sins into the depths of the sea" (Micah 7:18–19).

- "If we confess our sins, He is faithful and righteous to forgive us our sins and to cleanse us from all unrighteousness" (1 John 1:9).

Our nation has not fallen to the point where He cannot reach us. He can and will restore us to right standing if we call out to Him for forgiveness.

3. He will heal our land. Finally, God promises to restore us to wholeness and favor. This is important because of the wounds we face in our nation, including those that have been caused by people who sought to create divisions between us.

Think about the suspicion and skepticism we have toward our public officials, the bigotry exhibited by a great deal of the populace, and the political schisms that have been exploited at every turn. There is no longer unity of purpose or ideals. We no longer trust our fellow Americans.

James 4:1–4 explains the reason for these troubles:

> *What is the source of quarrels and conflicts among you? Is not the source your pleasures that wage war in your members? You lust and do not have; so you commit murder. You are envious and cannot obtain; so you fight and quarrel. You do not have because you do not ask. You ask and do not receive, because you ask with wrong motives, so that you may spend it on your pleasures. You adulteresses, do you not know that friendship with the world is hostility toward God? Therefore whoever wishes to be a friend of the world makes himself an enemy of God.*

We as a nation and as individuals have become too wordly, too concerned with our own desires. Now more than ever, we need the Father to heal our land. Be assured, He can restore us. If we obey Him, He will free us from our bondage. God—and only God—can unify us again. And, as Psalm 133:1 proclaims, "How good and how pleasant it is for brothers to dwell together in unity!"

LEARN FROM A KING WHO TURNED FROM PRIDE

Do you doubt that God can heal our land? That is understandable. Our country's challenges seem insurmountable at times. However,

Luke 18:27 reminds us, "The things that are impossible with people are possible with God."

Turn to the fourth chapter of the Book of Daniel, and you will find a leader so full of pride it seemed nothing could free him from it. We have discussed King Nebuchadnezzar before—how he had a dream no man could interpret and how he threatened to kill all of his advisors unless they could tell him what it meant. The Lord delivered Daniel and the other Jewish counselors by giving Daniel the wisdom he needed (see Daniel 2).

What we did not consider was Nebuchadnezzar's background, and we will now do so briefly. As we've seen, this man was absolutely vile, vicious, and tyrannical—willing to kill people on a whim (see Daniel 2) and burning them alive if they refused to obey him (see Daniel 3). Arguably the most significant monarch in Babylon's history, he reigned from approximately 605 to 562 BC, which means he was ruler of the nation while it was at the apex of its greatness.

In fact, months before he became king, Nebuchadnezzar gained fame on the worldwide stage by his striking victory at Carchemish over an Egyptian and Assyrian alliance. This victory made the Babylonian army the most powerful on earth at the time.

After he became king, he also reinforced his political influence by marrying Amytis (the daughter of Median King Cyaxares) and Nitocris (the daughter of Egyptian Pharaoh Necho II). For all intents and purposes, Nebuchadnezzar was at the top of the world. It seemed as if nothing could stop him.

It is no wonder, then, that the Lord sent Nebuchadnezzar a strong warning. Explaining the experience, the pagan king wrote,

> *I, Nebuchadnezzar, was at ease in my house and flourishing in my palace. I saw a dream and it made me fearful. . . . So I gave orders to bring into my presence all the wise men of Babylon, that they might make known to me the interpretation of the dream. . . . but they could not make its interpretation known to me. But finally*

Daniel came in before me . . . and I related the dream to him, saying . . . "[S]ince I know that a spirit of the holy gods is in you and no mystery baffles you, tell me the visions of my dream which I have seen, along with its interpretation. Now these were the visions in my mind as I lay on my bed: I was looking, and behold, there was a tree in the midst of the earth and its height was great. The tree grew large and became strong and its height reached to the sky, and it was visible to the end of the whole earth. . . . and behold, an angelic watcher, a holy one, descended from heaven. He shouted out and spoke as follows: 'Chop down the tree and cut off its branches, strip off its foliage and scatter its fruit. . . . Yet leave the stump with its roots in the ground . . . and let him share with the beasts in the grass of the earth. Let his mind be changed from that of a man and let a beast's mind be given to him, and let seven periods of time pass over him. This sentence is by the decree of the angelic watchers and the decision is a command of the holy ones, in order that the living may know that the Most High is ruler over the realm of mankind, *and bestows it on whom He wishes and sets over it the lowliest of men.'"* (Daniel 4:4–11, 13–17; *roman added for emphasis*)

Because Nebuchadnezzar did not understand what this meant, Daniel had the daunting task of telling him about the devastating nature of his pride—that he simply could not defy God and get away with it. The king had grown so strong and prominent throughout the earth that it was necessary for the Lord to humble him until he acknowledged the God of Heaven was the true Sovereign of all things.

Daniel pleaded with Nebuchadnezzar, saying, "Therefore, O king . . . break away now from your sins by doing righteousness and from your iniquities by showing mercy to the poor" (Daniel 4:27). Predictably, it was not long before Nebuchadnezzar completely forgot Daniel's admonition.

Daniel 4:29–32 reports,

> *Twelve months later he was walking on the roof of the royal palace of Babylon. The king reflected and said, "Is this not Babylon the great, which I myself have built as a royal residence by the might of my power and for the glory of my majesty?" While the word was in the king's mouth, a voice came from heaven, saying, "King Nebuchadnezzar, to you it is declared: sovereignty has been removed from you, and you will be driven away from mankind, and your dwelling place will be with the beasts of the field. You will be given grass to eat like cattle, and seven periods of time will pass over you until you recognize that the Most High is ruler over the realm of mankind and bestows it on whomever He wishes."*

Immediately, Nebuchadnezzar was driven from his palace, and for seven years he lived as an animal. The great king—the most powerful ruler of the earth—was reduced to grazing in the pasture with the cows.

God wasn't doing this to be cruel or spiteful. On the contrary, He was actually demonstrating grace and mercy to Nebuchadnezzar by revealing the sinfulness of his heart. The Lord understood it was necessary for this pagan king to hit rock bottom before he would acknowledge that every blessing he had received had come from God's hand (see James 1:17).

You see, pride must be exposed before we can be liberated from its hold. It was only when Nebuchadnezzar saw his true poverty that he could repent and give the Father the honor He was due.

Pride must be exposed before we can be liberated from its hold.

He said, "At the end of that period, I, Nebuchadnezzar, raised my eyes toward heaven and my reason returned to me, and I blessed the Most High and praised and honored Him who lives forever; . . . [A]ll His works are true and His ways just, and He is able to humble those who walk in pride" (Daniel 4:34, 37).

MOVE FROM PRIDE TO HUMILITY

Before we talk about developing a humble heart, there is one important thing I would like to clarify. When we speak about pride, there are two possible definitions.

The first is what we've been talking about: a focus on or inordinately lofty opinion of one's abilities and influence, which denies the need for God or accountability toward others.

The second is very different from the first. At times you will hear people say they take great pride in their children or their work. This refers to the personal joy and gratification we receive when something important turns out well. There is nothing ungodly about this. The Father wants us to give our finest efforts—to do our best, look our best, and be our best.

We know this because Colossians 3:23–24 instructs, "Whatever you do, do your work heartily, as for the Lord rather than for men, knowing that from the Lord you will receive the reward of the inheritance. It is the Lord Christ whom you serve."

God wants us to be sincere, enthusiastic, and wholehearted in our obedience to Him, and He wants us to do exceptional work for the sake of His name. This brings glory and pleasure to Him and should bring great satisfaction to our own hearts.

But we must understand that this second definition is not about seeing ourselves as better than others, but about giving our most excellent efforts in order to achieve something important.

When can we know we are being arrogant rather than just giving our best? When we begin to conclude, "I'm never wrong" or "I know everything there is to know about this subject," for example, conceit has taken control.

How do we root out these disastrous attitudes? By practicing the two statements that open the door for repentance and genuine forgiveness—expressions of a humble heart that help us to move toward greater wisdom.

- The first is simply, "I made a mistake."

- The second is, "I don't know."

Admit, "I Made a Mistake"

This first admission is a starting point in many important pursuits—including a personal relationship with God. First John 1:9 tells us, "If we confess our sins, He is faithful and righteous to forgive us our sins and to cleanse us from all unrighteousness."

This is the repentance that leads us to salvation. We realize we have no way to repay the penalty incurred by our transgressions, so we ask Jesus—who paid the cost in full on the cross—to do so for us.

Paul summarized this transaction in his letter to the Romans when he wrote, "The wages of sin is death, but the free gift of God is eternal life in Christ Jesus our Lord" (Romans 6:23).

There are other areas that must begin with acknowledging our mistakes as well—such as getting back on track as a nation. We must be willing to confess that we have not always demanded laws that honor the Lord, treated each other as He commands, or stood firm against the ungodly abuses of those in power.

When we are able to do this humbly before Him, He can then work to show us how to right the wrongs that have been done.

Admit, "I Don't Know"

The second admission is acknowledging not recognizing which course to take in order to stem the current tide and honor the Father. However, a profession of unawareness in this is, in itself, an excellent step.

A stumbling block for many people is that they simply don't realize what they don't know. There are areas of their understanding that are lacking—either because they have never been taught or because they've never before come upon a situation where that special knowledge set was necessary.

This is why it is absolutely essential for us to seek God in every decision, because only His wisdom is complete. It is only as He reveals the truth of a matter that we individually—and as a nation—can make crucial decisions.

One of the greatest examples of actively responding to God's Word was King Jehoshaphat of Judah. Word came to Jehoshaphat that his people and the capital city of Jerusalem were about to be attacked by the powerful allied armies of the Moabites, Ammonites, and Meunites. Jehoshaphat was terrified, and justifiably so. There was no way his army could hold off the invading hordes.

> It is absolutely essential for us to seek God in every decision, because only His wisdom is complete.

But he responded by doing exactly the right thing. He "turned his attention to seek the LORD, and proclaimed a fast throughout all Judah" (2 Chronicles 20:3).

People from all the cities of Judah gathered together at the temple, and Jehoshaphat stood in their midst, crying out to the Father for help. He prayed, "O LORD, the God of our fathers, are You not God in the heavens? And are You not ruler over all the kingdoms of the nations? Power and might are in Your hand so that no one can stand against You. . . . We are powerless before this great multitude who are coming against us; nor do we know what to do, but our eyes are on You" (2 Chronicles 20:6, 12).

Jehoshaphat had no idea how to handle the situation before him. He freely admitted his weakness before the Lord, and because of his humility, God showed Judah how to conquer those three powerful armies.

Notice that while our wisdom may have prescribed that every man, woman, and child in the nation pick up a sword and stand ready for combat, the Father's plan was very different. In fact, He did not want them to fight at all.

In the midst of the assembly the Spirit of the LORD came upon Jahaziel . . . and he said, "Listen, all Judah and the inhabitants of Jerusalem and King Jehoshaphat: thus says the LORD to you,

'Do not fear or be dismayed because of this great multitude, for the battle is not yours but God's. . . . You need not fight in this battle; station yourselves, stand and see the salvation of the LORD on your behalf, O Judah and Jerusalem.' Do not fear or be dismayed; tomorrow go out to face them, for the LORD is with you." And Jehoshaphat bowed his head with his face to the ground, and all Judah and the inhabitants of Jerusalem fell down before the LORD, worshiping the LORD. . . . They rose early in the morning and went out to the wilderness of Tekoa; and when they went out, Jehoshaphat stood and said, "Listen to me, O Judah and inhabitants of Jerusalem, put your trust in the LORD your God and you will be established. Put your trust in His prophets and succeed." When he had consulted with the people, he appointed those who sang to the LORD and those who praised Him in holy attire, as they went out before the army and said, "Give thanks to the LORD, for His lovingkindness is everlasting." When they began singing and praising, the LORD set ambushes against the sons of Ammon, Moab and Mount Seir, who had come against Judah; so they were routed. (2 Chronicles 20:14–15, 17–18, 20–22)

What a wonderful testimony of the Father's awesome power to save and deliver His people!

HEED THE CHALLENGE FOR OUR NATION

As a country, we can learn a great deal from this. There is nothing weak about admitting we don't have all the answers—as long as we couple it with a strong resolve to turn to God and believe He will help us.

After all, are we in less trouble than Jehoshaphat and the people of Jerusalem were? I think not. And God can rescue us as He did Jehoshaphat and the Judahites.

Our country has been hit with a tremendous number of extreme and costly disasters in recent years—from massive hurricanes, tornadoes, and floods, to a very serious oil spill.

We have endured the onslaught of terrorism—not only in the destruction of the Twin Towers of the World Trade Center in New York City on September 11, 2001, and the strike against the Pentagon in Washington, D.C., but also in the ongoing threat that requires us to be ever vigilant.

We have been devastated economically—with enormous losses in the banking, manufacturing, and real-estate sectors. We now have a tremendous national debt and considerable trade imbalances.

We are struggling to cope with the repercussions of illegal immigration and the massive influx of weaponry and drugs into our land.

We are facing ongoing international tensions—due to the wars we are involved in and because of nuclear threats against our allies.

The truth is we are absolutely powerless to deal with any of these crises in our own strength. It would be entirely appropriate for our lawmakers to call us to seek the Lord through serious fasting and prayer!

"But," some may say, "that is the responsibility of our country's pastors and evangelists." True. However, take note, Jehoshaphat was not a religious leader or the high priest. He was the king.

And Jehoshaphat received the direction he needed. What appeared to be an assault that would end in the destruction of Jerusalem turned out to be an event that built up the people's faith in God. It also resulted in a tremendous windfall—it took three days for the people of Judah to gather all the spoils from the camps of their enemies.

I readily admit I do not know how or if our nation will recover from all that is coming against us. But I do believe this: we must fast, pray, and trust the Lord for the answers. I have faith that what the Father has planned for our country is more wonderful than anything we can imagine (see Ephesians 3:20–21). We must simply believe that as we

We must fast, pray, and trust the Lord for the answers.

give Him our highest and most trusting allegiance, He will provide us with His best blessings.

DETERMINE TO TAKE THE PATH OF HUMILITY

Therefore, let us ask ourselves:

- Are we courageous enough to admit we have been wrong?

- Are we humble enough to acknowledge we do not understand which course to take?

- Are we willing to trust God to show us what to do?

- Are we prepared to obey Him—regardless of the consequences or whether we understand why He directs us to take a certain path?

The simple truth of the matter is that no one knows all the Father knows. No one sees the beginning from the end the way He does. But God will move heaven and earth to show us His will. We must simply be ready to follow Him whenever He calls.

Make no mistake, we *can* change things if we're willing to obey Him. So how do we begin? What can we do to turn the tide and seek God's path for our nation?

- We must pursue wisdom.

- We must speak up boldly for the truth and stand up to make a difference.

- And we must pray.

In the next four chapters, we will look more closely at the things we can and should do.

———————

Thank You, Lord, that You are always involved
in every aspect of our lives and that You are in control
of all things, at all times. Please forgive us for our pride.
Help us to have the courage to admit
we do not have all the answers
and have made mistakes.
Guide us into Your wisdom and teach us to do Your will.
We long to trust You completely in all things
and to follow You in obedience so
others can know You and be saved. Amen.

———————

HOW *YOU* CAN TURN THE TIDE

1. *"Before we ever consider the pride that plagues our leaders, we need to stop and take an honest look at our own hearts. Do we attribute the good things in our lives to our own power, abilities, and talents? Or do we recognize that they come from the Father? Do we acknowledge His sovereignty in all things?"*

Have you done as Dr. Stanley suggests? Have you taken an honest look at your own flaws before examining those of our leaders? What did you discover in your self-examination?

2. Dr. Stanley astutely points out: *"If God allows leaders who oppress us, pass ungodly laws, or are contrary to His values to take power, it may very well be He has done so to warn us things simply aren't right in our nation."*

What things are not right with our nation? What will you commit to doing to help turn the dangerous tide assaulting our country?

3. *"When Isaiah says the countries of the world are 'as a speck of dust on the scales,' it means they do not weigh anything at all to Him. He could hold all the continents of the earth in His hand and not even notice."*

What implications from this statement does Dr. Stanley draw? What new perspective does this Scripture verse give you about America? What might be in our future if we do not change our ways?

4. Dr. Stanley says that we must practice *"the two statements that open the door for repentance and genuine forgiveness—expressions of a humble heart that help us to move toward greater wisdom.*

- *The first is simply, 'I made a mistake.'*
- *The second is, 'I don't know.'"*

Do you have trouble with either of these statements? Think of a time when you didn't make one or both of these admissions. What do you miss out on when you don't make these acknowledgements? Will you ask God to humble you and enable you to make these admissions?

PART 3

TURNING THE TIDE

CHAPTER 10

THE TIDE-TURNING POWER
OF *WISDOM*

God's Word Is for Our Benefit,
Now and Always

Consider this: You are driving down the highway in the middle of the night. How do you ensure that your car will remain safely within the lane? You measure your progress by the center line, correct? As long as you keep your automobile aligned with the white or yellow stripe that runs down the middle of the street, you know where you are.

You also recognize that if you stay on your side of the road and the other drivers stay on theirs, you'll arrive safely at your destination.

But now imagine this: You are out in the country, it's midnight, and there are no streetlights. Suddenly, you realize there is no line in the center of the road to help you steer. You don't know where you are. You're just meandering because it's pitch dark and there's no guideline to direct you.

Individuals and countries who make decisions based on their own preferences rather than established, absolute truth are like drivers on a highway with no center line. Their situation and circumstances change—as do their desires and values. As a result, there is nothing consistent and sure by which they can make their choices. There is no real direction or guidance for their personal lives or for national decisions.

As believers, we should have basic principles we live by—convictions we form as we grow in our intimate relationships with God through reading His Word and through prayer. This is because we exist for a cause much greater and more important than we are. We're living for Jesus Christ and for His kingdom, bearing witness to who He is in our lives. If we want to be effective citizens who are instrumental in turning the dangerous tide that is beseiging our nation, we must first be very clear in our minds as to what we believe and how we live out those beliefs. Proverbs 4:4–13 teaches,

> *"Let your heart hold fast my words;*
> *Keep my commandments and live;*
> *Acquire wisdom! Acquire understanding!*
> *Do not forget nor turn away from the words of my mouth.*
> *Do not forsake her [wisdom], and she will guard you;*
> *Love her, and she will watch over you.*
> *The beginning of wisdom is: Acquire wisdom;*
> *And with all your acquiring, get understanding.*
> *Prize her, and she will exalt you;*
> *She will honor you if you embrace her.*
> *She will place on your head a garland of grace;*
> *She will present you with a crown of beauty."*
> *Hear, my son, and accept my sayings*
> *And the years of your life will be many.*
> *I have directed you in the way of wisdom;*
> *I have led you in upright paths.*
> *When you walk, your steps will not be impeded;*
> *And if you run, you will not stumble.*
> *Take hold of instruction; do not let go*
> *Guard her, for she is your life.*

In other words, the wisdom we find in Scripture is our center line—keeping, directing, and safeguarding us in every situation and circumstance. It is our anchor in times of storm, regardless of the tempest assailing us. This is why it is so important for us to take the Father's commands seriously.

> The wisdom we find in Scripture is our center line—keeping, directing, and safeguarding us in every situation and circumstance.

GOD'S WORD REVEALS HIS NATURE

The reality is that there is no greater expression of truth than the Word of God. It is the written record of the Lord's unfolding revelation of His ways, character, nature, and saving love.

Isaiah 40:8 teaches, "The grass withers, the flower fades, but the word of our God stands forever." In other words, life has its ebb and flow, comings and goings, births and deaths; but Scripture remains absolutely fixed because it is based on the One who is unchanging (see Hebrews 13:8). The Bible's truth never varies, and by no means ever will. It is inspired, infallible, inerrant, incomparable, inimitable, and indestructible.

The apostle Paul tells us, "All Scripture is inspired by God and profitable for teaching, for reproof, for correction, for training in righteousness; so that the man of God may be adequate, equipped for every good work" (2 Timothy 3:16–17). This is absolutely true. Scripture is a powerful tool the Father uses not only to transform our personal lives but to guide us daily as we seek to influence our nation. How does He do so?

1. The Word of God Affirms That He Will Rescue Us in Times of Need

For example, we can read David's testimony and be assured the Lord will help us overcome our problems. In Psalm 57:2–3 he writes, "I will cry to God Most High, to God who accomplishes all things for me. He will send from heaven and save me; He reproaches him who tramples upon me. God will send forth His lovingkindness and His truth." David endured great pressures all of his life, yet he confidently declared that the Lord is faithful to rescue His people.

2. The Bible Reminds Us of God's Awesome Promises

Sometimes we simply need to be reminded that the Father is with us—that we are guaranteed His presence (see Deuteronomy 31:6, 8), wisdom (see Jeremiah 33:3), strength (see Zephaniah 3:17), and provision (see Philippians 4:19) in every circumstance. How absolutely encouraging it is to read, "Blessed be the LORD . . . not one word has failed of all His good promise" (1 Kings 8:56).

3. Scripture Instructs Us in the Way We Should Go

Growing up, I studied the stories of the Old Testament about how the Father worked in the lives of faithful men such as Abraham, Moses, Joshua, David, and Daniel. I learned the truth of Romans 15:4: "Whatever was written in earlier times was written for our instruction, so that through perseverance and the encouragement of the Scriptures we might have hope." In other words, if you and I are obedient to the Lord as they were, we will experience a life of significance and victory—which really is life at its very best.

4. God's Word Reveals the Father's Character and Activity

If we wish to grow deeper in our relationships with the Father, we must understand His perspective, attributes, and ways. We must know Him better and grow in our love for Him. We must also learn to walk in the center of His will.

David realized this, which is why he sought God with all his heart. And he was able to testify:

The LORD my God illumines my darkness.
For by You I can run upon a troop;
And by my God I can leap over a wall.
As for God, His way is blameless;
The word of the LORD is tried;
He is a shield to all who take refuge in Him.
For who is God, but the LORD?
And who is a rock, except our God,
The God who girds me with strength
And makes my way blameless?
He makes my feet like hinds' feet,
And sets me upon my high places. (Psalm 18:28–33)

The truth of the matter is, the Bible is like no other book ever written. Sir Isaac Newton once said, "If all the great books of the world were given life and were brought together in Convention, the moment the Bible entered, the other books would fall on their faces." This is because there is no competition for its profound subject, truth, depth, wisdom, beauty, or accuracy. It transcends time, helps us to see the Father's eternal plan throughout history, and infuses our lives with purpose.

> The Bible is like no other book ever written. There is no competition for its profound subject, truth, depth, wisdom, beauty, or accuracy.

There are absolutely no detriments in knowing and obeying the Word of God. There are only benefits!

SCRIPTURE CALMS THE ANXIOUS HEART

We can be assured that the Holy Spirit works through God's Word to comfort us in times of hardship, and that includes the challenges our nation is facing. To truly comprehend this, we must think about what it would mean to go through trials and difficulties without the assurance we find in His Word.

Without the testimony of Scripture, our times of trouble would seem meaningless—without any redemptive quality. We would have no powerful and loving Source of help and would potentially go looking for assistance in all the wrong places. We would have no hope of our pain ever ending or our situations changing. And the problems we face could ultimately tear us down—devastating us and leaving us insecure, bitter, resentful, fearful, depressed, and completely miserable.

However, because we have God's Word and accept it as true, we know:

1. The Father works through our difficulties for our good (see Romans 8:28).

2. There is a purpose for the adversity we face (see Romans 5:3–5; James 1:2–4; 1 Peter 1:6–7).

3. We can always seek the Lord to help us, no matter what we face (see Psalms 40:1–4; 91:4–9; Isaiah 30:18–21; 41:9–10; John 16:33).

4. The dark moments of our lives will last only as long as it takes for the Father to teach us what He desires us to learn (see Genesis 37–45).

5. If we trust and obey God, we will not only overcome our problems, but they will prepare us for even greater triumphs and maximum usefulness (see Romans 8:31–37; 2 Corinthians 12:7–10).

It is a tremendous blessing to have hope and to live without fear as we experience personal hardships and national problems. However, this hope is only possible if we pay close attention as we read Scripture and listen to the Holy Spirit as He brings His life-giving truth to our minds. We must have faith in what He reveals to us and not doubt; because the Word of God is powerful, and He will use it to transform our lives if we permit Him.

> **The Word of God is powerful, and He will use it to transform our lives if we permit Him.**

In Psalm 19:7–11 David affirmed the following:

The law of the LORD is perfect, restoring the soul;
The testimony of the LORD is sure, making wise the simple.
The precepts of the LORD are right, rejoicing the heart;
The commandment of the LORD is pure, enlightening the eyes.
The fear of the LORD is clean, enduring forever;
The judgments of the LORD are true; they are righteous
   altogether.
They are more desirable than gold, yes, than much fine gold
Sweeter also than honey and the drippings of the honeycomb.
Moreover, by them Your servant is warned;
In keeping them there is great reward.

SCRIPTURE GUIDES A NATION'S LEADERS

As you probably recall, David faced an immense amount of pressure throughout his life. But because of all the adversity he faced, he learned he could completely depend upon God and trust His Word. The result of David's time with the Father and meditating on Scripture was that he became—for the most part—the ruler Israel needed.

The Word of God has always been absolutely indispensible for leaders—especially those who lead His people. In fact, all the kings of Israel were commanded to read the Book of the Law every day. Deuteronomy 17:18–20 instructs:

> *"When he [the king] sits on the throne of his kingdom, he shall write for himself a copy of this law on a scroll in the presence of the Levitical priests. It shall be with him and he shall read it all the days of his life, that he may learn to fear the LORD his God, by carefully observing all the words of this law and these statutes, that his heart may not be lifted up above his countrymen and that he may not turn aside from the commandment, to the right or the left, so that he and his sons may continue long in his kingdom in the midst of Israel."*

Likewise, when Joshua became leader of Israel, he was commanded:

> *"Be strong and very courageous; be careful to do according to all the law which Moses My servant commanded you; do not turn from it to the right or to the left, so that you may have success wherever you go. This book of the law shall not depart from your mouth, but you shall meditate on it day and night, so that you may be careful to do according to all that is written in it; for then you will make your way prosperous, and then you will have success."*
> *(Joshua 1:7–8)*

Why were they instructed to give such importance to Scripture?

1. Because Leadership Is Both Difficult and Lonely

These leaders needed to be in the Word constantly in order to re-member that the Father had not abandoned them but had guaranteed they would ultimately be victorious. When they focused on the character of God and the promises He had made—instead of their temporary defeats—they found the strength to persevere.

2. Because Meditating on Scripture Keeps Leaders Centered on the Father's Goals

Read any book on leadership, and you will see the indispensible necessity of concentrating your efforts on the objective and not being distracted by peripheral issues. When you and I spend time reading and studying the Bible, we are focused on the Lord's primary goal for our lives, which is to draw us into an intimate relationship with Himself, and thereby conforming us to the image of Christ (see Romans 8:29).

3. Because Leaders Face Challenges They Cannot Conquer in Their Own Strength

Both Joshua and David faced armies and enemies they could not possibly overcome without God's intervention. You see, Scripture not only reveals who the Lord is, but also teaches us the truth about ourselves as human beings and about the world as a whole. These men needed to understand the tactics their enemies could use against them, the Father's ability to thwart their plans, and the way He wanted them to proceed through each and every circumstance.

4. Because Leaders Set the Moral and Spiritual Tone of the Nation

As they encountered moral and ethical dilemmas, both Joshua and David had to be godly examples to their people and act in a manner that honored God.

In all these things, Scripture helps us as well. By keeping us focused on the Father's character and promises, we are likewise able to triumph over times of loneliness and difficulty, we remain centered on the goals He has for us, we are able to face very difficult circumstances in His strength, and we become an example of His godly grace to others.

GOD'S WORD IS A WISE COMPASS FOR OUR LIVES

This leads us to the next point, which is that Scripture is a compass for our lives, directing us in the way we should go. In Psalm 119:9–12, David wrote:

> *How can a young man keep his way pure?*
> *By keeping it according to Your word.*
> *With all my heart I have sought You;*
> *Do not let me wander from Your commandments.*
> *Your word I have treasured in my heart,*
> *That I may not sin against You.*
> *Blessed are You, O LORD;*
> *Teach me Your statutes.*

Regrettably, many people seem to have a desire to live in a "gray zone"; they don't want to worry about the concepts of right and wrong. They often make statements such as these:

- "Surely the Father understands how much better this makes me feel."

- "The Bible is old-fashioned; it doesn't really apply to today's world."

- "The Lord doesn't really expect us to be perfect."

These people like to think of themselves as godly; but in truth, they have chosen a cafeteria-style faith—picking and choosing what they want to believe. They do not really stand in awe of holy God, and because they don't, they cannot develop the mature character of Jesus that they were created to enjoy.

Yes, the Lord understands why we sin. In fact, Jesus shared in our humanity in order to comprehend the struggles we face (see Hebrews 2:14–18). But He also realizes that our transgressions lead to our destruction. He doesn't want us to face the terrible consequences of our iniquities. Rather, He desires for us to live a joyful life of forgiveness and fulfillment.

This is why God's Word tells us there is an absolute standard for right and wrong. Repeatedly, Scripture warns us to turn away from evil and pursue wisdom and godliness.

- "Do not be wise in your own eyes; fear the LORD and turn away from evil. It will be healing to your body and refreshment to your bones" (Proverbs 3:7–8).

- "He who is steadfast in righteousness will attain to life, and he who pursues evil will bring about his own death" (Proverbs 11:19).

- "The one who despises the word will be in debt to it, but the one who fears the commandment will be rewarded" (Proverbs 13:13).

- "Will they not go astray who devise evil? But kindness and truth will be to those who devise good" (Proverbs 14:22).

- "The way of the wicked is an abomination to the LORD, but He loves one who pursues righteousness" (Proverbs 15:9).

- "The highway of the upright is to depart from evil; he who watches his way preserves his life" (Proverbs 16:17).

In fact, Proverbs 1:29–32 addresses those who reject the Lord and refuse to obey Him, painting a dreadful picture of what their lives will be like:

> *"Because they hated knowledge*
> *And did not choose the fear of the LORD.*
> *They would not accept my counsel,*
> *They spurned all my reproof.*
> *So they shall eat of the fruit of their own way*
> *And be satiated with their own devices.*
> *For the waywardness of the naive will kill them,*
> *And the complacency of fools will destroy them."*

Frankly, I cannot envision a worse way to live. This is a portrait of those who refuse to listen to wisdom or to have a center guideline for their lives. They will receive the punishments that accompany their sins—being filled to overflowing with their consequences and despair. They will get themselves into situations that cause their ruin with no opportunity for rescue, because they utterly refuse any deliverance the Father offers them.

What a helpless, hopeless existence—and for what? For the promise of immediate pleasure that does not last, but turns sour even as they are partaking of it. Selfish, sinful living is always foolish.

What a difference from the godly. Proverbs 1:33 affirms, "He who listens to me shall live securely and will be at ease from the dread of evil."

If you and I truly want to live without fear in our innermost being, we must listen to the Lord—through prayer and by reading His Word.

In other words, if you and I truly want to live without fear in our innermost being, we must listen to the Lord—through prayer and by reading His Word. We must go to Him with open hearts, paying close attention to all His instructions. As we read Scripture, we must ask the Holy Spirit to apply it to our lives, revealing His solutions and wisdom for the decisions we must make.

Then, as He shows us how to proceed, we should do as instructed in Proverbs 3:5–6: "Trust in the LORD with all your heart and do not lean on your own understanding. In all your ways acknowledge Him, and He will make your paths straight."

PUT GOD'S WORD INTO YOUR LIFE

As you diligently work to put God's Word into your life, it will become an anchor in times of storm and a center line to navigate by, just as it was for David and Joshua. Over time, you will begin to learn the Father's viewpoint, ways, and wisdom, because you will have a deeper understanding of His holy character.

Then, because of your time in His presence, you will start to emulate His love, joy, peace, patience, kindness, gentleness, faithfulness, and self-control toward others—showing them mercy and forgiveness as He would. In other words, by learning about God and spending quality time with Him, you will become increasingly like Jesus in your thoughts, words, and deeds (see Galatians 5:22–23).

This is why it is so important that you read the Bible today and every day and allow its principles to transform your spirit, attitudes, words, and actions. By doing so, you will not only strengthen your faith but also develop the courage to express your convictions.

But, you may be thinking, *I don't really understand everything the Bible says and means. What do I do?* My response is twofold:

1. Buy a Bible in a Translation or Version That You Comprehend

Not everyone is comfortable with the language of the *King James Version*, and that is all right. I personally prefer the *New American Standard Bible* (NASB). Also, I often read *The Living Bible* (TLB) because it is very easy to absorb. There are many excellent versions, but be sure the one you choose is accepted by mainstream evangelical Christianity. The most important thing, however, is not the translation, but that you are actively engaging with and applying Scripture to your life.

2. Just Start Reading—and Do It Daily

The God who saved you is also able to teach you how to live in a manner that is pleasing to Him. The Holy Spirit will speak to your heart about what the Word says—instructing you how to deal with the challenges and issues you are currently experiencing. If you're prepared to listen to and accept His counsel, He is always willing to show you what to do.

If you are consistent and dedicated in your Bible reading, over time you'll discover how passages relate to one another, and the Father's truth will be established in an awesome way in your life. Of course, this does not happen overnight. The Word of God is a bottomless ocean of wisdom for you to explore.

> **The Word of God is a bottomless ocean of wisdom for you to explore.**

In fact, I have read through the Bible more times than I can count, and each time is an adventure. The Father always reveals inspiring new principles and nuggets of truth for me to meditate on, study, and preach. It's simply awesome how He speaks through His Word!

My hope and prayer is that you experience this as well. Therefore, I challenge you to:

- read God's Word *regularly*.

- study your Bible and meditate on its principles *thoroughly*.

- believe Scripture *wholeheartedly*.

- apply God's Word *personally*.

- obey His commands *faithfully*.

- share the gospel message *boldly*.

- defend the truth of Scripture *courageously*.

- live out the principles of God's Word *consistently*.

- give away the Bible *generously*—by literally providing copies of Scripture to others and by teaching it to whomever you meet.

When you do these things, the Lord will give you such breathtaking insights that you will be filled with awe, joy, and wonder. And before you know it, He will also bring about genuine change in the way you think, speak, and act.

SCRIPTURE—THE STANDARD OF GOD'S BEST FOR THE NATION

Why have we gone into such an extensive discussion of God's Word in a book about good citizenship? Because if we want the country to head in the right direction, we must first know where the center line is. We must understand the important principles our nation must align with—and be sure we are living by them—before we can voice our opinion about what must change.

As noted previously, 1 Peter 4:17 tells us, "It is time for judgment to begin with the household of God." As members of the Body of Christ, we

> If we want the country to head in the right direction, we must first know where the center line is.

must measure our behavior against the standards of Scripture. When we identify sin in our lives, we must confess it to the Lord and trust Him to teach us how to live according to His will.

The following passage is one I often find myself praying. I encourage you to meditate on its words and use it in your time alone with the Father.

I am Your servant; give me understanding,
That I may know Your testimonies.
It is time for the LORD to act,
For they have broken Your law.
Therefore I love Your commandments
Above gold, yes, above fine gold.
Therefore I esteem right all Your precepts concerning everything,
I hate every false way.
Your testimonies are wonderful;
Therefore my soul observes them.
The unfolding of Your words gives light;
It gives understanding to the simple.
I opened my mouth wide and panted,
For I longed for Your commandments.
Turn to me and be gracious to me,
After Your manner with those who love Your name.
Establish my footsteps in Your word,
And do not let any iniquity have dominion over me.
(Psalm 119:125–133)

I pray these verses minister to your soul as they do mine. I also hope that you've been moved to approach God's Word in a new, more fervent, and more powerful manner, because our country is absolutely desperate for godly men and women like you to lead the way.

The good news is that when you and I seek Him, the Father *will* reveal what to do. And we can be absolutely certain that when He does, it will be the very best path for the transformation of our nation (Matthew 7:7–11).

So will you dig into Scripture and discover what the Father desires to do in and through your life? Will you be like David and Joshua, meditating on the Word of God daily in order to lead your fellow countrymen in a manner that is godly and pleasing to the Lord?

It's not too late. Open its pages and embrace its wisdom.

Almighty God, please give us a hunger for Your wisdom,
and a thirst for Your righteousness.
Drive us to Your Word
so we might discover anew Your plans
and purposes for our lives and for our nation.
Give us a longing for Your very best,
and help us keep in the very center of Your will
and perfectly aligned to Your principles. Amen.

HOW *YOU* CAN HELP TURN THE TIDE

1. *"It is so important that you read the Bible today and every day . . . by doing so, you will not only strengthen your faith but also develop the courage to express your convictions."*

How are you doing with your personal Bible reading and study? How can the strength you gain by regular Bible study help you do your part to turn the tide of our nation?

2. *"We must understand the important principles our nation must align with—and be sure that we are living by them—before we can voice our opinion about what must change."*

According to Dr. Stanley's statement above, what responsibilities do we have before we can begin speaking out for specific change? Why is this important?

3. Dr. Stanley asks the very pointed question *"Will you dig into Scripture and discover what the Father desires to do in and through your life?"*

How would you answer Dr. Stanley? Are you currently digging into God's Word on a regular basis? What have you discovered in Scripture about what the Father wants to do in and through your life?

CHAPTER 11

THE TIDE-TURNING POWER OF *SPEAKING THE TRUTH BOLDLY*

We Have a Right and Responsibility to Stand for God

A s we discussed in the previous chapter, if we want our country to head in the right direction, we must first know that our center line is based on Scripture. We should understand the important biblical principles our nation must align with and make sure we're living by them before voicing our opinion about what ought to change.

But once we know the truth, we have a responsibility to speak it out boldly and act on it with confidence.

When I think about this principle, a very stirring story from the life of Paul comes to mind. He was in the midst of his third missionary journey when the Father called him to go back to Jerusalem and then on to Rome (Acts 19:21). Yet he knew it would in no way be an easy visit. While in Miletus, he asked the elders from the church at Ephesus to come there and meet with him. He told them:

"You yourselves know, from the first day that I set foot in Asia, how I was with you the whole time, serving the Lord with all humility and with tears and with trials which came upon me through the

plots of the Jews; how I did not shrink from declaring to you anything that was profitable, *and teaching you publicly and from house to house, solemnly testifying to both Jews and Greeks of repentance toward God and faith in our Lord Jesus Christ. And now, behold, bound by the Spirit, I am on my way to Jerusalem, not knowing what will happen to me there, except that the Holy Spirit solemnly testifies to me in every city, saying that bonds and afflictions await me.* But I do not consider my life of any account as dear to myself, so that I may finish my course and the ministry which I received from the Lord Jesus, to testify solemnly of the gospel of the grace of God." *(Acts 20:18–24; roman added for emphasis)*

Here is a man who gave himself totally to the Lord Jesus. Once the apostle Paul understood the Father's will, he absolutely refused to back away from it. Even though there were those who warned him of the trials he would suffer and begged him not to go to Jerusalem, Paul would not be dissuaded from his path (Acts 21:4, 10–12). He boldly told them, "What are you doing, weeping and breaking my heart? For I am ready not only to be bound, but even to die at Jerusalem for the name of the Lord Jesus" (Acts 21:13).

> "I do not consider my life of any account as dear to myself, so that I may finish my course and the ministry which I received from the Lord Jesus, to testify solemnly of the gospel of the grace of God."—Acts 20:24

Are we as committed as he was? If not, then we should be. Paul was willing to endure anything—including execution—for the sake of the gospel. Why? Because he loved God and knew how very important it was to tell people how to be saved. He also realized the eternal ramifications of being faithful to the Lord's calling. We must do so as well.

NOW IS THE TIME

More than ever in our history, it is time to speak up for what we know is right, good, and beneficial. There is nothing to be gained by our silence—but there is much to be lost.

Asaph called God's people to recognize the truth of their condition in the following psalm, and we must do the same. We must admonish and encourage our fellow Americans to confront the reality of our times.

The passage below is a bit long, but as you read through it, I encourage you to circle the words and phrases you believe apply to our national condition today. It will be well worth your time and thought.

Surely God is good to Israel,
To those who are pure in heart!
But as for me, my feet came close to stumbling,
My steps had almost slipped.
For I was envious of the arrogant
As I saw the prosperity of the wicked.
For there are no pains in their death,
And their body is fat.
They are not in trouble as other men,
Nor are they plagued like mankind.
Therefore pride is their necklace;
The garment of violence covers them.
Their eye bulges from fatness;
The imaginations of their heart run riot.
They mock and wickedly speak of oppression;
They speak from on high.
They have set their mouth against the heavens,
And their tongue parades through the earth.

Therefore his people return to this place,
And waters of abundance are drunk by them.
They say, "How does God know?
And is there knowledge with the Most High?"
Behold, these are the wicked;
And always at ease, they have increased in wealth.
Surely in vain I have kept my heart pure
And washed my hands in innocence;
For I have been stricken all day long
And chastened every morning.
If I had said, "I will speak thus,"
Behold, I would have betrayed the generation of Your children.
When I pondered to understand this,
It was troublesome in my sight
Until I came into the sanctuary of God;
Then I perceived their end.
Surely You set them in slippery places;
You cast them down to destruction.
How they are destroyed in a moment!
They are utterly swept away by sudden terrors!
Like a dream when one awakes,
O Lord, when aroused, You will despise their form.
When my heart was embittered
And I was pierced within,
Then I was senseless and ignorant;
I was like a beast before You.
Nevertheless I am continually with You;
You have taken hold of my right hand.
With Your counsel You will guide me,
And afterward receive me to glory.
Whom have I in heaven but You?
And besides You, I desire nothing on earth.
My flesh and my heart may fail,

But God is the strength of my heart and my portion forever.
For, behold, those who are far from You will perish;
You have destroyed all those who are unfaithful to You.
But as for me, the nearness of God is my good;
I have made the Lord GOD my refuge,
That I may tell of all Your works. (Psalm 73)

As we read Asaph's words, we see his honest discouragement, his observations, and his thought processes that brought him back to faith in God. It is easy for the Father's most faithful people to become discouraged—especially when it seems as if ungodly people are succeeding in their plans. They may ask, doesn't God care? Why is He allowing His people to suffer? Isn't He listening to the prayers of His people? Why does He allow evil men to prosper?

Yet we are assured the Lord *does* hear and answer our cries for His help. Any prosperity experienced by the ungodly is merely temporary. The Father's ways of establishing His justice may be beyond our abilities to comprehend, but we can be confident He is working.

Therefore, God must be the strength of our hearts and our portion forever. Even though there will be times when it is uncomfortable to share the gospel and we may feel as if we're not qualified to lead others to Him, we must proceed with the understanding that He is with us. His presence energizes and equips us for everything He desires for us to do.

> "God is the strength of my heart and my portion forever."
> —Psalm 73:26

INFLUENCE AS SALT AND LIGHT

In a very practical sense, we must decide whether we wish to *impress* people or *impact* their lives—allowing God to work through us to transform them.

So many people in our society do everything they can so that others will admire and envy them. They spend a great deal of money, dress a certain way, drive expensive cars, and live in prominent neighborhoods. It's obvious to everyone around them that their main goal is to impress. However, when our goal is for the Lord to influence lives through our testimonies, our interactions with others will take on a completely different dynamic.

When you think about having an *impact* on a person's life, it indicates a collision, of sorts. What you say, how you live, and your very presence cause them to rethink their lives, prompting them to change. Or, as Proverbs 27:17 says, "Iron sharpens iron, so one man sharpens another."

> **What you say, how you live, and your very presence cause them to rethink their lives, prompting them to change.**

In fact, Jesus taught that we have an absolute responsibility to influence those around us. He said:

> *You are the salt of the earth; but if the salt has become tasteless, how can it be made salty again? It is no longer good for anything, except to be thrown out and trampled under foot by men. You are the light of the world. A city set on a hill cannot be hidden; nor does anyone light a lamp and put it under a basket, but on the lampstand, and it gives light to all who are in the house. Let your light shine before men in such a way that they may see your good works, and glorify your Father who is in heaven.* (Matthew 5:13–16)

It is God's will for every single believer to live in such a way that we impact the people around us. One of the big mistakes we make as the Body of Christ is that we sing, pray, and read the Bible together but often neglect to practice what we've learned in a concrete way. We think that if we fulfill our role as the church within the walls of the building, that is enough. However, Jesus was clear. He said

"*Go* therefore and make disciples of all the nations" (Matthew 28:19, italics added). *Attending* church is excellent—and we should all do it—but it is not enough. The Savior also calls us to *go* forth. The people we talk to, listen to, and work with should see a difference in our lives—we should be sharing all that God teaches us with them.

So what does being salt and light mean to us personally? Let us look at them individually.

> *Attending* church is excellent—and we should all do it—but it is not enough. The Savior also calls us to *go* forth.

The Salt of the Earth

Salt was an extremely valuable commodity in the ancient world for many reasons. It was used as an antiseptic, a preservative, a sign of hospitality, a seasoning (influencing/affecting taste), and a confirmation of a covenant, among other things.

In the life of a believer, it is symbolic for many similar qualities:

Preservation. In ancient times, before refrigeration, salt was used to keep meat from spoiling. As Christians, we safeguard—or preserve—people in two ways. First, God may work through our testimonies to influence others to accept Jesus as Lord and Savior—preserving them for eternity. Second, as we teach others to live a godly life, we help them avoid the destructive consequences of sin—protecting their lives and witness on the earthly level.

Seasoning. Salt also makes a difference by changing the taste of food. Likewise, as believers, we change situations by our very presence because the Holy Spirit dwells in us. According to the Beatitudes in Matthew 5:1–11, we are to be humble, thoughtful, gentle, righteous, merciful, pure, peace-making, firm in our faith, and focused on the higher purpose of God's kingdom. These attributes have a tremendous impact, regardless of the circumstances. People see how different we are and the tranquility, confidence, and security we bring, even in the midst of turmoil. They want us around because we make their lives better.

Influence. It doesn't take much salt before a dish is fully affected by its flavor. That's how a godly life is to be: people cannot help but want to emulate it and have it for themselves. When we've been with Jesus, His love, wisdom, power, and character flow through our lives, drawing people to a relationship with Him. Of course, when they accept Christ as their Savior, the same thing becomes true of their lives. Then *they* become the kind of person others love to be around and want to emulate. The influence of the Lord's presence in and through us spreads and continually affects every soul it touches.

The Light of the World

Additionally, you and I are to be beacons of the gospel's truth—reflecting Christ's glory faithfully. Jesus said, "I have come as Light into the world, so that everyone who believes in Me will not remain in darkness" (John 12:46).

Likewise, the apostle Paul also admonishes, "Prove yourselves to be blameless and innocent, children of God above reproach in the midst of a crooked and perverse generation, among whom you appear as lights in the world" (Philippians 2:15). What qualities of light does Paul want us to emulate?

Light illuminates the way. Many people are living in spiritual darkness and enduring great difficulties. They are desperate to have something to cling to—someone to help them find a path to peace. They would accept Christ as their Savior if we would just sit down and illuminate the way to Him.

Light reveals the truth. The truth of the matter is, people are apt to conceal the things they are ashamed of or afraid of. Sometimes they hide their sins and wounds so well, they no longer acknowledge—even to themselves—that they exist. Yet those issues and transgressions are very present, affecting every decision made. However, the Holy Spirit often works through us to expose what is buried deep within and the bondage experienced. Our conduct and character can convict people of their sinfulness. And our wholehearted confidence and trust in the Father may make them aware of the peace they are lacking.

WHEN SALT AND LIGHT COLLIDE WITH THE WORLD

As you might imagine, our presence as salt and light will not always make other people feel comfortable. On the contrary, the very fact that we are trying to impact their lives means we are on a collision course with them.

This is why 2 Peter 3:15–17 admonishes:

Sanctify Christ as Lord in your hearts, always being ready to make a defense to everyone who asks you to give an account for the hope that is in you, yet with gentleness and reverence; and keep a good conscience so that in the thing in which you are slandered, those who revile your good behavior in Christ will be put to shame. For it is better, if God should will it so, that you suffer for doing what is right rather than for doing what is wrong.

The apostle Paul likewise wrote, "Let no unwholesome word proceed from your mouth, but only such a word as is good for edification according to the need of the moment, so that it will give grace to those who hear. . . . Be kind to one another, tender-hearted, forgiving each other, just as God in Christ also has forgiven you" (Ephesians 4:29, 32).

We must be people of principle, patience, faith, courage, and humility. We must strive to ensure that our response to others is filled with the Holy Spirit's power—is overflowing with His love, wisdom, and authority. We never want our words or conduct to be the reason anyone rejects Jesus.

> **We never want our words or conduct to be the reason anyone rejects Jesus.**

However, we must also decide to stand up, speak out, and be courageous in the hopes of leading others to salvation and influencing the course of our country.

We should be strong examples and advocates of responsibility and accountability. This means encouraging one another to be good citizens, living debt-free, and modeling honest, moral lives. And we must pray without ceasing, lift up the name of Jesus so others can know the hope within us, and praise God in every situation—knowing He is working on our behalf.

POWERFUL TOOLS AT OUR DISPOSAL

Thankfully, as believers, we have important tools at our disposal to transform our country and reach our fellow Americans. We have:

1. the love, wisdom, and strength of the Lord.

2. the Word of God.

3. the power of prayer.

4. our example as we live in obedience to the Father.

5. our influence with others.

6. the privilege of voting our values.

7. our civic right to run for office and shape the political discourse.

These tools will be especially important in the elections we face in the years to come. We must learn to use them in the most effective way possible.

Of course, you may think most believers already know how to utilize the rights and privileges God has given us. However, I recently read a report which indicated that almost half of all Bible-believing, evangelical Christians are not currently registered to vote—even in some of the most important battleground states in our nation.

Although we have a system that fully allows us to be involved in deciding the direction of the country, believers are forfeiting their rights to influence the course it takes. This is to our detriment—because, as we know, ungodly forces never give up an opportunity to take control.

The more we keep silent about the wrongs in our nation, the further we will lose our ability to speak out about them in the future. Friend, this is why it is absolutely crucial that Christians vote every time we are given the opportunity.

OF CHARACTER AND CANDIDATES

Please notice, I have not suggested which party anyone should support, and I am not going to. That is between the individual and God. But if you are not already involved, I will strongly recommend you take note of what's happening in this country and engage in the civic discourse.

I also advise that we pay close attention to the character of each of the nominees running for public office. Integrity is one of the most important qualities an elected official can have. Therefore, we should always look for verifiable and

> We should always look for verifiable and objective evidence that our candidates exhibit the moral fiber that we expect of them.

objective evidence that our candidates exhibit the moral fiber we expect of them.

Here are some questions we can ask of not only our lawmakers but also all of our leaders:

- Does the person consistently tell the truth and act in an honest and principled manner?

- Is the individual reliable, faithful, and trustworthy, doing as he says he will—including honoring his marital and family commitments?

- Does the person give generously to others—especially to those in need?

- Does the individual exhibit sound, ethical reasoning— including protecting the sanctity of life and the traditional definition of marriage?

- Is the individual conscientious about paying her bills and taking care of her financial obligations?

- Does the person speak respectfully to others, with kindness, consideration, and gentleness?

- Is the individual humble, treating others with dignity and appreciation?

- Does the person consistently extend common courtesies to others?

- Is the individual careful—reviewing all of her options and the ramifications of her decisions with due diligence?

- Does the person exhibit self-control in his habits?

- Is the individual willing and prepared to be an example, living by the same standards he or she sets for others?

- Does the person know how to have fun and make others laugh without resorting to coarse joking, crude language, or inappropriate stories?

- Does the individual exhibit patience as others learn new information and tasks, or is he easily irritated?

- Is the person a peacemaker—seeking to resolve arguments and find quality solutions?

- Does the individual encourage and inspire others to become better people?

- Does the person express any remorse for mistakes and exhibit sincere attempts to make amends and do what is right?

- Is the individual modest—not pointing to her own achievements but focusing on the needs and accomplishments of others?

- Does the person work well with others and exhibit good judgment—making decisions that demonstrate wisdom and fairness?

- Is the individual prepared to stand up for the truth, no matter what it costs?

I'm sure you can add other questions. However, please note how very important it is that we observe our candidates' behaviors instead of just listening to their words. Although you can learn a great deal by examining a legislator's website or campaign literature, actions are far more reliable indicators of a person's character than words can or ever will be.

This goes for us as well. You and I must always be people who exhibit godliness and character in everything we say and do. What we articulate does no good if our behavior contradicts our words.

> What we articulate does no good if our behavior contradicts our words.

A CALL TO GODLY ACTION

At the beginning of this chapter, we observed the courage of the apostle Paul and how he was willing to die for the sake of the gospel if necessary. This characteristic was not unique to him—the disciples were just as committed to obeying God as he was. They lived to testify about all Jesus had done for them and to lead others to the Savior. Some even gave their lives.

Peter and the other apostles of the early church were often arrested by religious leaders, who were intensely jealous of their success in healing the sick, casting out unclean spirits, and attracting new believers. In one such instance reported by Acts 5, we're told, "During the night an angel of the Lord opened the gates of the prison, and taking them out he said, 'Go, stand and speak to the people in the temple the whole message of this Life.' Upon hearing this, they entered into the temple about daybreak and began to teach" (Acts 5:19–21).

The apostles gladly obeyed—even though they understood that they would more than likely end up right back in jail. They did not worry about what others thought or about their personal safety. They only cared that God had called them and that there were people who needed to hear about salvation through Jesus Christ.

Of course, the high priest and the other members of the Council were infuriated when they heard the prisoners had escaped and were back in the temple preaching. Immediately, they rearrested the disciples. Acts 5:27–32 tells us the story:

> *The high priest questioned them, saying, "We gave you strict orders not to continue teaching in this name, and yet, you have filled Jerusalem with your teaching and intend to bring this man's blood upon us." But Peter and the apostles answered, "We must obey God rather than men. The God of our fathers raised up Jesus, whom you had put to death by hanging Him on a cross. He is the one whom God exalted to His right hand as a Prince and a Savior, to grant repentance to Israel, and forgiveness of sins. And we are witnesses of these things; and so is the Holy Spirit, whom God has given to those who obey Him."*

There was absolutely no way these faithful believers would stop speaking about Christ. They couldn't. They knew if they did, people would die in their sins and spend eternity separated from the Father. Notice how they addressed their persecutors. They did not belittle the Jewish leaders; instead, they preached the gospel to them. The apostles spoke out so that the Sadducees judging them would know how to have forgiveness of their sins through the death and resurrection of Jesus Christ.

> "We must obey God rather than men."—Acts 5:29

Always remember, the greatest way for you and me to fight unrighteousness is to speak out for the righteousness that can only be gained through a personal relationship with Jesus.

Sadly, the religious leaders did not repent. Acts 5:33 tells us they "were cut to the quick and intended to kill" the disciples. However, a wise man

> The greatest way for you and me to fight unrighteousness is to speak out for the righteousness that can only be gained through a personal relationship with Jesus.

named Gamaliel stopped them from doing so—and the counsel he gave them was very interesting. He said, "Stay away from these men and let them alone, for if this plan or action is of men, it will be overthrown; but if it is of God, you will not be able to overthrow them; or else you may even be found fighting against God" (Acts 5:38–39).

Even more amazing, the Jewish leaders accepted this rabbi's recommendation. After beating the disciples, they released them.

APPLYING THE PRINCIPLE
TO OUR LIVES

We should take Gamaliel's advice to heart as well. No man can thwart the Lord's plans (see Job 42:2; Psalm 33:11; Isaiah 14:27). This is one of the many reasons you and I should be faithful and obedient to Him. Because when we're in the center of His will, we're on the path to ultimate success.

The disciples understood this, which is why "they went on their way from the presence of the Council, rejoicing that they had been considered worthy to suffer shame for His name. And every day, in the temple and from house to house, they kept right on teaching and preaching Jesus as the Christ" (Acts 5:41–42).

Too many believers today lack this courage. They avoid telling others about Jesus or revealing their faith because they dread the repercussions. And they do not stand for morality and truth in our country because they do not wish to be seen as religious zealots.

Friend, we can no longer afford to cater to these fears. We no longer have the luxury of merely trying to impress people. We have a responsibility to boldly declare the truth we have learned and to act on it with confidence. Like the disciples, we must fight unrighteousness by proclaiming the salvation that is given to us freely through a personal relationship with Jesus Christ.

For some, this signifies running for public office. For others, it means writing letters to representatives, speaking out publically about certain issues, and taking a more active role in civil matters.

But for *all* believers, this means obeying God in whatever He asks us to do. It also indicates we must make the most of our privilege as American citizens by voting.

We have been called to impact people's lives as salt and light. Therefore, we must focus on helping those around us find the path to eternal life through the Savior, rather than worrying about their temporary, earthly opinions.

And we must obey God, rather than men.

Many people we meet are on a collision course—just as our country is. Will we allow them to be destroyed by the world or help them and our nation be strengthened by the truth?

Both you and I realize which path we must take.

———————

Give us courage, Lord, to speak up
and stand for what is right in Your sight.
Teach us Your words for Your people,
and may our words pierce their hearts with Your truth.
Help us to be salt and light so many will know You as Savior.
Show us, Lord, who deserves our vote.
Help us elect the men and women
You desire to work through in the coming years.
And Father, show us how to honor You above men
and stand courageously in the face of opposition.
You are the strength of our hearts
and our portion forever.
To You be all the honor, glory, power, and praise. Amen.

———————

WHAT *YOU* CAN DO TO TURN THE TIDE

1. *"More than ever in our history, it is time to speak up for what we know is right, good, and beneficial. There is nothing to be gained by our silence—and much to be lost."*

Dr. Stanley calls us to action in the statement above. If you are not actively involved in speaking up for what you know is right for our country, write down three specific things you can do along with a timeline of when you'll do them. Then you'll be on your way to helping turn the tide that is threatening to overwhelm us.

2. *"We must decide whether we wish to* impress *people or* impact *their lives."*

The above statement from Dr. Stanley refers to an issue that affects every single one of us. Understanding your own personal motivation in any situation requires some honest heart evaluation and prayer. Ask God to give you insight into your heart and to guide you in purifying your motives. Then you will be a tool He can use.

3. *"We must strive to ensure that our response to others is filled with the Holy Spirit's power—is overflowing with His love, wisdom, and authority. We never want our words or conduct to be the reason anyone rejects Jesus."*

Standing up and speaking out is vital to the health of our nation. But honoring Christ is even more important. How about you? Are you standing up and speaking out in a way that evidences the Holy Spirit within you?

CHAPTER 12

THE TIDE-TURNING POWER OF *PRAYER*

Doing the Will of Heaven on Earth

I t began with a small group of people who were members of the historic Saint Nicholas Church in Leipzig, East Germany—or the German Democratic Republic (GDR), as it was officially called back then. They met on Mondays at 5:00 p.m. to cry out to God, uttering *Friedensgebete*, or Prayers for Peace, for their nation—a country devastated by the failures and oppression of communism. These prayer warriors also read the Sermon on the Mount in unison, allowing it to guide their behavior and claiming the promises in it:

> *Blessed are the poor in spirit, for theirs is the kingdom of heaven.*
> *Blessed are those who mourn, for they shall be comforted.*
> *Blessed are the gentle, for they shall inherit the earth.*
> *Blessed are those who hunger and thirst for righteousness, for they*
>   *shall be satisfied.*
> *Blessed are the merciful, for they shall receive mercy.*
> *Blessed are the pure in heart, for they shall see God.*
> *Blessed are the peacemakers, for they shall be called sons of God.*
> *Blessed are those who have been persecuted for the sake of*
>   *righteousness, for theirs is the kingdom of heaven.*

Blessed are you when people insult you and persecute you, and
falsely say all kinds of evil against you because of Me.
Rejoice and be glad, for your reward in heaven is great.
(Matthew 5:3–12)

This prayer group, which started in 1982 with only six members, was small for years. But by 1988 that had changed, and intercessors began meeting daily. The group grew and moved to a larger room of the church, then to the largest chamber, and finally to the main sanctuary.

In fact, by May 1989, the gathering had become so numerous that GDR authorities became concerned and tried to restrict access to the church. They also sent secret police officials of STASI (*Ministerium für Staatssicherheit* or Ministry for State Security) to attend the meetings; they threatened those who had come to pray and imprisoned many.

But this did not dissuade the prayer warriors. They continued to meet and cry out to God for the nation. By October, more than two thousand people inside the church and ten thousand outside were holding candles and praying—undeterred by communist pressure. Though GDR police and soldiers were sent to silence them, the intercessors refused to respond violently—instead clinging to the message of the Sermon on the Mount and praying faithfully.

The Communists were intent on censoring the growing movement, but, as we learned in the previous chapter, no one can thwart that which begins with the Lord. The rabbi Gamaliel taught, "If it is of God, you will not be able to overthrow them; or else you may even be found fighting against God" (Acts 5:39). And that is exactly what happened. The more the East German government persecuted the people, the more people joined to petition the Father for the future of the nation.

> **"If it is of God, you will not be able to overthrow them; or else you may even be found fighting against God."—Acts 5:39**

One month later, on November 9, 1989, the Berlin Wall came down.

The twelve-foot-high concrete barrier that symbolized the absolute tyranny of communism was destroyed.

On June 26, 1963, in his famous speech to the people of West Berlin, President John F. Kennedy aptly described the awful oppression the wall represented. He said,

There are many people in the world who really don't understand, or say they don't, what is the great issue between the free world and the Communist world. Let them come to Berlin. There are some who say that communism is the wave of the future. Let them come to Berlin. And there are some who say in Europe and elsewhere we can work with the Communists. Let them come to Berlin. And there are even a few who say that it is true that communism is an evil system, but it permits us to make economic progress. . . . Let them come to Berlin. Freedom has many difficulties and democracy is not perfect, but we have never had to put a wall up to keep our people in, to prevent them from leaving us. . . . The wall is the most obvious and vivid demonstration of the failures of the Communist system, for all the world to see . . . as your Mayor has said, an offense not only against history but an offense against humanity, separating families, dividing husbands and wives and brothers and sisters, and dividing a people who wish to be joined together.

Yet when believers cried out to God, just look how He was able to work through their prayers! East Germany was freed from communist rule and families were reunited after decades of separation. Truly, "The effective prayer of a righteous man can accomplish much" (James 5:16).

A TIME FOR PRAYER

The time has come for *us* to pray—as the faithful intercessors of Saint Nicholas Church in Leipzig did—believing the Father can mightily reverse the tide assailing our nation. The truth of the matter is, when we fight our battles on our knees, we win every time.

When we fight our battles on our knees, we win every time.

Take Nehemiah, for example. He was cupbearer to the powerful King Artaxerxes I, who reigned in Persia from circa 465 BC to 425 BC. In his role, Nehemiah would not only have a high place at court—as one of the only servants allowed to remain when the queen was present—but he would also be deeply trusted by the king. After all, Artaxerxes counted on Nehemiah to ensure his wine was not poisoned.

Like Daniel, Nehemiah's family had undoubtedly been brought to the region during one of the three deportations from Judah to Babylon, which lasted from 605 BC to 586 BC. As we saw in the story of Daniel, life was often difficult for the people under Babylonian rule. However, things changed in 539 BC when the Persian King Cyrus conquered the Babylonians.

As prophesied by both Isaiah (see 44:28; 45:1–6) and Jeremiah (see 25:12; 29:10), Cyrus decreed,

> *"The LORD, the God of heaven, has given me all the kingdoms of the earth and He has appointed me to build Him a house in Jerusalem, which is in Judah. Whoever there is among you of all His people, may his God be with him! Let him go up to Jerusalem which is in Judah and rebuild the house of the LORD, the God of Israel; He is the God who is in Jerusalem." (Ezra 1:2–3)*

So, after seventy years of exile, the Jews were permitted to return to their land.

Sadly, in the more than ninety years from the time that the Jewish people began emigrating back into Jerusalem (circa 537 BC) until the time of Nehemiah (circa 445 BC), very little had been done to restore the wall. The city remained in ruins. Nehemiah wrote,

It happened . . . that Hanani, one of my brothers, and some men from Judah came; and I asked them concerning the Jews who had escaped and had survived the captivity, and about Jerusalem. They said to me, "The remnant there in the province who survived the captivity are in great distress and reproach, and the wall of Jerusalem is broken down and its gates are burned with fire."

When I heard these words, I sat down and wept and mourned for days; and I was fasting and praying before the God of heaven. I said, "I beseech You, O LORD God of heaven, the great and awesome God, who preserves the covenant and lovingkindness for those who love Him and keep His commandments, let Your ear now be attentive and Your eyes open to hear the prayer of Your servant which I am praying before You now, day and night, on behalf of the sons of Israel Your servants, confessing the sins of the sons of Israel which we have sinned against You; I and my father's house have sinned. We have acted very corruptly against You and have not kept the commandments, nor the statutes, nor the ordinances which You commanded Your servant Moses. Remember the word which You commanded Your servant Moses, saying, 'If you are unfaithful I will scatter you among the peoples; but if you return to Me and keep My commandments and do them, though those of you who have been scattered were in the most remote part of the heavens, I will gather them from there and will bring them to the place where I have chosen to cause My name to dwell.' They are Your servants and Your people whom You redeemed by Your great power and by Your strong hand. O Lord, I beseech You, may Your ear be attentive to the prayer of Your servant and the prayer of Your servants who delight to revere Your name, and make Your servant successful today and grant him compassion before this man." (Nehemiah 1:1–11)

Nehemiah was heartbroken when he learned about the condition of the wall and the few people who were left in Jerusalem. But he understood that if he truly wanted the situation to change, he would have to pray and obey—no matter what it cost him.

FIGHTING THE BATTLE ON OUR KNEES

You may be asking, *How did Nehemiah's prayer show him what to do?* Through his time on his knees, Nehemiah learned the awesome, unlimited power of God to work through any situation. By praying, Nehemiah aligned himself with the Father's will. So when Artaxerxes asked him what was wrong, Nehemiah had the words, courage, wisdom, and favor to explain the problem to the king and receive the help he needed (see Nehemiah 2:1–8).

This does not mean Nehemiah's task was stress-free and simple once he reached Jerusalem. On the contrary, he experienced tremendous challenges and obstacles. However, he always sought the Father's guidance and strength, regardless of the danger or difficulty he faced, and was able to prevail because of His provision.

Through the power and wisdom of the Lord and Nehemiah's godly leadership, the people of Jerusalem were able to rebuild the wall in just fifty-two days (Nehemiah 6:15)—a task they had previously been unable to accomplish for ninety years!

LEARNING HOW TO PRAY

This account about Nehemiah may sound amazing, but that's how the awesome power of God works. As Ephesians 3:20 confirms, He "is able to do far more abundantly beyond all that we ask or think." His capacity to deliver us from all of our difficulties is above and beyond our comprehension and imagination.

As you and I spend time in worship and intercession, we learn about the Lord's ability to overcome whatever difficulties we may face. Prayer is the tool of choice God has given us to communicate with Him—to reach out for His wisdom, to plead our case before Him, and to receive everything we require from His gracious hand.

> God's capacity to deliver us from all of our difficulties is above and beyond our comprehension and imagination.

So, how do we pray?

1. Start by Recognizing the Father Is Sovereign and Holy

If we do not have an accurate comprehension of who the Lord is, we will never truly understand how absolutely astounding the privilege of prayer is. This is why it is so crucial that we develop our intimate relationship with God—embracing His wisdom, power, majesty purity, and love. Just by reading David's inspiring words of praise, we know that he understood the power and majesty of God:

> *"Blessed are You, O LORD God of Israel our father, forever and ever. Yours, O LORD, is the greatness and the power and the glory and the victory and the majesty, indeed everything that is in the heavens and the earth; Yours is the dominion, O LORD, and You exalt Yourself as head over all. Both riches and honor come from You, and You rule over all, and in Your hand is power and might; and it lies in Your hand to make great and to strengthen everyone. Now therefore, our God, we thank You, and praise Your glorious name." (1 Chronicles 29:10–13)*

2. Understand the Lord's Majesty and Righteousness

This understanding will naturally lead us to confession and repentance. When Isaiah was given a vision of God on His throne, in the fullness of His glory, the prophet was completely overcome. He exclaimed, "Woe is me, for I am ruined! Because I am a man of unclean lips, and I live among a people of unclean lips; for my eyes have seen the King, the LORD of hosts" (Isaiah 6:5).

Like Isaiah, when you and I enter into the presence of the Father and realize how absolutely holy and sovereign He is, we may sometimes feel overwhelmed by His presence and convicted of our sinfulness. We shouldn't fear experiencing this or become discouraged when we understand how far we fall short of the Lord's holiness. It is quite natural for us to realize how vastly weak, inadequate, and flawed we are before Him.

Rather, the Father reveals our transgressions and frailties to us so that we will confess them and learn to rely upon Him.

Therefore, when we pray, we should humble ourselves before the Father, and ask Him to cleanse us of our sin. We can pray as David did, "Create in me a clean heart, O God, and renew a steadfast spirit within me. Do not cast me away from Your presence and do not take Your Holy Spirit from me. Restore to me the joy of Your salvation and sustain me with a willing spirit" (Psalm 51:10–12).

3. Express Our Willingness to Be Used in the Lord's Service

It is amazing how being in God's sovereign presence and experiencing freedom from sin motivates us to serve Him out of love and thankfulness. This is exactly what happened to Isaiah. After he was cleansed from his unrighteousness, he "heard the voice of the Lord, saying, 'Whom shall I send, and who will go for Us?'" Isaiah immediately responded, "Here am I. Send me!" (Isaiah 6:8).

This is because the Father's presence energizes us for our work. He reveals Himself to us for the specific purpose of encouraging, enabling, strengthening, invigorating, informing, or warning us. We are then motivated to honor and serve Him wholeheartedly.

4. Submit to God's Timing, Purpose, Power, and Direction

We must always heed God's commands whether we understand them or not. Are we available for the Lord? Are we willing to drop what we are doing in order to obey what He is calling us to do? Are we prepared to surrender ourselves completely to His plans for achieving His purposes?

This is often the most difficult part for us because it means bringing our own will and desires under submission. When the Father calls us to a task, are we willing to say yes to Him? Too often, when circumstances do not develop as we expect them to—taking longer than we thought they should or proceeding in an unexpected direction—we begin to question God's will. We wonder if we heard Him correctly or if we should try to figure it out on our own.

During these times it is crucial for us to remember that it isn't necessary for us to understand what the Father is doing—it is only crucial that we obey Him. We must remain faithful in prayer, realizing the Lord will reveal His path and provision for us at just the right time.

INTERCEDING FOR OUR LEADERS

You may be thinking, *Learning to pray is wonderful, but is there a way I can intercede specifically for our leaders? Isn't it important to lift each of them up to the Father because of their significant role in our country?*

Yes it is. Praying for the men and women who develop, pass, and enforce the laws of our nation is absolutely crucial. The apostle Paul admonished Timothy:

> *I urge that entreaties and prayers, petitions and thanksgivings, be made on behalf of all men, for kings and all who are in authority, so that we may lead a tranquil and quiet life in all godliness and*

dignity. This is good and acceptable in the sight of God our Savior, who desires all men to be saved and to come to the knowledge of the truth. (1 Timothy 2:1–4)

Following are ten specific things that I encourage you to pray for regarding those who are in leadership in your life and in government.

1. Pray that the Lord will cause people in authority to realize their sinfulness and daily need for Jesus' forgiveness and guidance.

2. Pray that our legislators will admit their personal inadequacies for the tasks ahead and turn to the Father for the wisdom and courage to carry out their responsibilities.

3. Pray that our lawmakers will reject all counsel that violates the spiritual principles set forth in Scripture, and that they will trust God to lead them in the best direction.

4. Pray that our government officials will be able to resist pressure from those who would lead them astray or tempt them to violate the will of God and the clear standards of right and wrong.

5. Pray that those in authority will actively work to reverse the trends in our nation that dethrone the Lord and deify man.

6. Pray that our leaders be willing to abandon their political careers and personal ambitions if doing so is in the best interests of the country.

7. Pray that our representatives will rely upon prayer and the Word of God for their daily strength and path to success.

8. Pray that our legislators will restore dignity, honor, trustworthiness, and righteousness to our government and their offices.

9. Pray that our lawmakers will strive to be good examples to all the parents and children in our nation.

10. Pray for all people in authority to be reminded daily that they are accountable to Almighty God for their attitudes, words, motives, and actions.

CHANGE THEM OR REMOVE THEM

Make no mistake; our prayers on behalf of the leaders in our nation can be very powerful and effective. Remember the promise of Proverbs 21:1, "The king's heart is like channels of water in the hand of the LORD; He turns it wherever He wishes." When we cry out to the Father, He can influence our lawmakers in astounding ways.

A friend of mine can testify to this fact. Some years ago, he was part of a group of Christians in his company who banded together to intercede for the success of the business. They asked the Lord to direct the leadership, giving wisdom and insight to everyone in positions of authority—from first-line supervisors to the chairman of the board. Once a week, they met during their lunch break, fasting and crying out for the Father's intervention.

He told me, "Our prayer for the leaders of our company boiled down to this one statement: 'Change 'em or remove 'em, Lord!'"

"Did it happen?" I asked.

"Again and again," he said. "Often the transformation happened quickly—almost overnight. In many cases, people suddenly retired or resigned. They were with us one week and gone the next. But a few had a radical change of heart. They never revealed the reasons why they were approaching their coworkers and duties so differently, but we knew that God was working."

"What was the long-term result?"

<blockquote>"We knew that God was working."</blockquote>

"Over a period of about three years, godly behavior became much more prevalent in our company. We saw improved morale, as well as an increase in productivity, efficiency, and quality. Sales soared. Profits multiplied. Our jobs were more secure than ever. Also, our workplace became much more respectful and kind."

What a wonderful testimony—one that we would like to see repeated in every office, community, and state in our nation.

"Change 'em or remove 'em, Lord," is an effective prayer regarding any elected official who ignores God's commands. Our first desire is to see them enjoy the eternal life Jesus freely provided for us. But if they will not acknowledge the Savior, we can ask the Father to help them find another occupation.

JOIN IN FAITH AND PRAYER WITH OTHERS

As I've continually maintained throughout this book, you and I can change this country. We can be like Nehemiah and the intercessors at Saint Nicholas Church, who fought their battles on their knees and saw the Father's awesome victory in their situations.

In Mark 11:22–24, Jesus affirmed, "Have faith in God. Truly I say to you, whoever says to this mountain, 'Be taken up and cast into the sea,' and does not doubt in his heart, but believes that what he says is going to happen, it will be granted him. Therefore I say to you, all things for which you pray and ask, believe that you have received them, and they will be granted you."

With such a wonderful promise from our Savior, why wouldn't we pray? We would be crazy not to! So let's intercede on behalf of our nation—both as individuals and with other like-minded believers.

For example, if there is someone you trust to share your concerns about your family, friends, work, church, city, and nation; ask him or her to be your prayer partner. However, because of the intensity and intimacy that prayer partners experience, I advise men to pray with other men and women with other women.

I also encourage you to participate in opportunities such as the National Day of Prayer, which always takes place on the first Thursday of May. Join other Christians in interceding for the country and offering thanks and praise to God for all the ways He has blessed America.

Finally, give serious consideration to either joining or starting a prayer group. Jesus said, "If two of you agree on earth about anything that they may ask, it shall be done for them by My Father who is in heaven. For where two or three have gathered together in My name, I am there in their midst" (Matthew 18:19–20). There is power when we gather together to intercede for our country because Jesus Himself is there praying with us. And there is nothing more awesome than that.

Of course, you may be thinking, *I'm willing to join a group, but I'm not exactly sure what to pray.* Look back to the ten prayer points for leaders we discussed just a few pages ago for some specific guidelines. Also, you will find a general prayer guide in the next chapter to assist you.

Just remember, you do not have to be fancy or eloquent in your prayers. Simply talk to your Father in heaven, and He will do the rest.

If the Lord can overcome the deeply ingrained communism of East Germany and work through the intercession of believers to knock down the Berlin Wall . . . and if He can empower a cupbearer to organize the people of Jerusalem and rebuild the wall and gates of the city in just fifty-two days . . .

He can certainly help us.

So let us pray. And let us give our awesome God all of the glory.

Lord God, bring us to our knees as a nation.
Teach us to pray, Father.
Show us Your power, love, and wisdom as we bow before You.
Father, we have faith that You can move mightily
and that You will do awesome things
as we humble ourselves before You.
We know You will show us what to do,
Please give us the strength and knowledge to carry out
Your marvelous plans.
Draw us close to You and
help us to intercede for our country and leaders.
We look to You and count on Your grace today and every day.
Amen.

WHAT *YOU* CAN DO TO
TURN THE TIDE

1. *"The time has come for* us *to pray—as the faithful intercessors of Saint Nicholas Church in Leipzig did—believing that the Father can mightily reverse the tide assailing our nation."*

What about the story of the church in Leipzig touched you the most? Drawing from their example, what are you willing to do to help reverse the tide assailing our nation?

2. *"The Father's presence energizes us for our work. He reveals Himself to us for the specific purpose of encouraging, enabling, strengthening, invigorating, informing, or warning us, which then motivates us to honor and serve Him wholeheartedly."*

How have you been energized by God's presence? How did you use the energy He gave you to honor and serve Him? If you haven't experienced this supernatural energizing and motivation, pray and ask God to reveal to you how He wants you to serve Him.

3. *" 'Change 'em or remove 'em, Lord,' is an effective prayer regarding any elected official who ignores God's commands."*

For whom do you need to pray this prayer? Will you commit to praying diligently and expectantly for God's moving in this person's life?

PART 4

THE PATHWAY TO REAL CHANGE

CHAPTER 13

PRAY ABOUT THE ISSUES WE FACE

A Twenty-Week Prayer Guide

A s we discussed in chapter 10, the Father promises, "If . . . My people who are called by My name humble themselves and pray and seek My face and turn from their wicked ways, then I will hear from heaven, will forgive their sin and will heal their land" (2 Chronicles 7:13–14). So in July of 2010, I called upon those in my church and all of our In Touch Ministries partners to intercede very specifically on behalf of our nation for twenty weeks—which is 140 days.

Within hours after I issued this challenge on the broadcast, our website crashed and our phone lines were jammed because of all the people who contacted us to say, "I'll join you in prayer!" Along with our Impact Prayer Team, more than a hundred thousand brothers and sisters in Christ joined together to make a difference in our country by getting on their knees before the Lord.

It was absolutely powerful! So many faithful believers crying out to God for their fellow citizens—asking Him to turn the spiritual tide and save the people of our land. We cannot imagine all the awesome things the Father began to do through all those

> We cannot imagine all the awesome things the Father began to do through all those saints whose hearts were set on Him.

saints whose hearts were set on Him—and what He is still doing. I am positive that a great deal of how the Father is answering our prayers is yet to be seen. The possibilities are completely beyond comprehension.

Therefore, I wanted to share the following guide with you, because it represents the issues and areas we covered in prayer:

- WEEK 1: Personal Preparation

- WEEK 2: God's Ability to Help Us

- WEEK 3: The Church's Recognition of Its Responsibility

- WEEK 4: Our Fellow Americans

- WEEK 5: Revival and Spiritual Awakening

- WEEK 6: God's Intervention to Turn the Tide

- WEEK 7: The Financial Crisis

- WEEK 8: Increasing Taxation

- WEEK 9: Increasing Unemployment

- WEEK 10: The Rapid Erosion of Our Liberties

- WEEK 11: Confusion and Corruption

- WEEK 12: The War Against Jesus

- WEEK 13: Terrorism

- WEEK 14: Turning Away from Israel

- WEEK 15: Reaffirming Our Nation's Christian Heritage

- WEEK 16: The Unborn

- WEEK 17: The Biblical View of Marriage

- WEEK 18: Natural Disasters

- WEEK 19: Worldwide Revival

- WEEK 20: Praise to God for What He Will Accomplish

Certainly this list of prayer concerns for our nation is not complete. It is, however, an excellent starting point. So I invite you to intercede on behalf of your fellow Americans and see what the Lord will do.

WEEK 1: PERSONAL PREPARATION

Pray for personal preparation, repentance, obedience, steadfastness, and faith during this time of national and spiritual crisis. As you begin to pray for our nation, it is important that you prepare your own heart first—going before the Father and making sure you have no unfinished business with Him. Revival and spiritual awakening in our land begin with you and all of us as believers—the church of Jesus Christ.

Therefore, ask the Lord to help you repent of your sinfulness, obey Him steadfastly, and be strong in your faith so you can be His powerful representative to and prayer warrior for this country.

> Revival and spiritual awakening in our land begin with you and all of us as believers—the church of Jesus Christ.

Be gracious to me, O God, by examining my heart and revealing my sins. According to Your loving-kindness and the greatness of Your compassion, show me where I have strayed from Your will so I may confess my transgressions to You and know the freedom of Your forgiveness. Make me clean before You so I can intercede with an open and contrite heart for my nation. The people of America need You, Lord—we need You to open our eyes and hearts to Your truth. Thank You for beginning to change this country by transforming my own heart. Thank You for hearing my prayer. In Jesus' name, Amen. (See Psalm 51.)

WEEK 2: GOD'S ABILITY TO HELP US

Pray for God to remind us how He has answered prayer in the past. We can move forward with confidence in praying for our nation because we know how faithfully God has responded to His people in the past. There is absolutely no obstacle or challenge He is unable to overcome. Although there are days we may feel the problems on the horizon are too great to conquer, we must rely on the fact that our heavenly Father is all-knowing, perfectly powerful, always with us, and completely loving.

There is absolutely no obstacle or challenge God is unable to overcome.

Therefore, let us praise Him, because He is capable of turning around our circumstances and showing Himself powerful on our behalf.

Lord God Almighty, I thank You that You will not reject us forever. Thank You for showering Your loving-kindness on us as we humble ourselves, seek Your face, and repent of our sins. I remember Your deeds of old, Father, and I meditate on all the wonders You performed for those who trusted You. I know there is nothing we will ever face as a nation that You cannot deliver us from—for who is great like You, O my God? Who has clothed His people with strength or provided for us as perfectly as You? By Your power, Lord, I ask You to redeem this country and make Your glory known to us. Thank You for transforming our country and for hearing my prayer. In Jesus' name, Amen. (See Psalm 77:7–15.)

WEEK 3: THE CHURCH'S RECOGNITION OF ITS RESPONSIBILITY

Pray for God to open the eyes of the church so that we and our fellow Christians can recognize our responsibility to intercede for the nation. The Lord has called us as believers to be His representatives to the world—not only on an individual level, but also corporately as the Body of Christ. Therefore, it is only right that as we pray for our nation, we ask God to restore the church to what He created her to be, working through her to bring this country back to Himself.

As we've discussed several times, 1 Peter 4:17 admonishes, "It is time for judgment to begin with the household of God." For our country to change, we know the church must experience revival. Please pray that the Body of Christ will recognize its own sinfulness and responsibility before the Lord and respond to Him in obedience.

Father, I thank You for calling us Your own. We are Your people, the Body of Christ. We humbly ask Your forgiveness, Lord, because You made us to be the salt of the earth—but in many ways, we have lost our flavor. Even though we still carry so much darkness within us, by Your power we can be a light to our nation and this world. Help us to accept and faithfully fulfill our responsibility as Your representatives on earth—not only by preaching the gospel, but by living in complete obedience to You. Help us shine our light before men in such a way that they will receive Jesus Christ as their Savior and glorify You, Lord.

> "It is time for judgment to begin with the household of God."
> —1 Peter 4:17

We accept that judgment begins with the church, Father, so please cleanse us and make us worthy ambassadors for the sake of Your name. Thank You for transforming this country by first reviving the church. And thank You for hearing my prayer. In Jesus' name, Amen. (See Matthew 5:13–16.)

WEEK 4: OUR FELLOW AMERICANS

Pray for God to open the eyes of Americans to the need for His intervention in our country. What we truly need in this nation is a spiritual awakening—for our fellow Americans to understand that true freedom and salvation can only be found through the Lord Jesus Christ. This week, please pray that as God draws the hearts of unbelievers in this country, they will be open to asking questions about Christ and hearing the good news of the gospel. Pray also that they will respond in faith to the Lord's call and commit to obeying Him in every area of their lives—including being His representatives as they fulfill their responsibilities as citizens of the United States.

Lord God, surely You are good to those who obey You. But Father, I confess my heart is broken because of the prosperity of the wicked and the deceptiveness of riches. So many in this nation envy the wealthy, believing they experience no problems or pain. Pride, anger, and covetousness fill their hearts, and they do not understand the hope You offer. They set their mouths against You, mocking Your law and the ways of Your people. They run after possessions and pleasures that will devastate rather than satisfy them.

Father God, please help the lost to realize the end that awaits them if they stay on this path—that they will be cast down to destruction. Help them to comprehend that the only true hope is in You—the only true wealth is salvation through Jesus Christ. When their flesh and hearts fail, may they seek You as their strength and portion forever.

Do not allow them to perish, Father. Show them how good it is to trust You as their refuge. Speak through Your people. Help us to tell of Your wonderful works so that people across this country will trust You as Lord and Savior and will walk in all Your ways. Thank You for redeeming my fellow Americans and hearing my prayer. In Jesus' name, Amen. (See Psalm 73.)

WEEK 5: REVIVAL AND SPIRITUAL AWAKENING

Continue to pray for spiritual awakening and revival throughout the nation. Revival and spiritual awakening usually go hand-in-hand. As the Bride of Christ (the church) is restored in her relationship with Jesus Christ, she becomes more evangelistic and missions-minded. Believers reach out in love and hope to their families, friends, co-workers, and community members—preaching the gospel and meeting needs. Meanwhile, the Holy Spirit stirs the hearts of the lost, showing them that something very important is missing in their lives that no earthly substance or object can satisfy.

Unbelievers see the revived activity of the church and are spiritually awakened to their own longing for a relationship with the living God. Therefore, please continue to pray for revival and spiritual awakening in our nation, and ask the Holy Spirit to provide divine appointments for Christians to lead the lost to salvation in Jesus Christ.

> Pray that unbelievers see the revived activity of the church and are spiritually awakened to their own longing for a relationship with the living God.

Lord God Almighty, revive us again that Your people may rejoice in You! Show us Your loving kindness—let it flow through us, Father, so others in our country may be awakened to their need for salvation. Help us to hear Your voice, and direct us by Your Holy Spirit. Please speak unity and peace to us, Your people, so that we may carry the Good News of Jesus Christ to those who are lost and perishing. Let us not turn back to folly, Father—destroying our testimonies to the people around us. Help us carry Your message with loving-kindness, truth, righteousness, and gentleness.

We ask You to prepare the hearts of the lost to accept Your salvation. Awaken unbelievers to their desire for Your presence, and help them understand it is only available through the death and resurrection of our Lord Jesus Christ.

Give us divine appointments wherever we go, Father—that we may preach Your gospel and that many will be saved. Indeed, Lord, You always give what is good, and Your Word never returns void—it always yields its produce. By Your Holy Spirit, guide our footsteps to those who long to know You, and give us the words they need to hear. Thank You for bringing revival and spiritual awakening to our nation. I praise You for hearing my prayer. In Jesus' name, Amen. (See Psalm 85:6–13.)

WEEK 6: GOD'S INTERVENTION TO TURN THE TIDE

Pray for God to change the direction of the destructive spiritual tide that is engulfing our nation. As you think about the devastating tide that is fast approaching our country, it is good to call to mind God's promise to us in Psalm 32:6, "Let everyone who is godly pray to You in a time when You may be found; surely in a flood of great waters they will not reach him." The Lord *can* turn this tide—and you *will* find Him if you truly seek Him.

The question is, have you really taken what it means to pray for revival and spiritual awakening to heart? Have you rid your life of all sin and apathy? Have you committed to living in obedience to the Father? Consider these things as you ask the Lord to change the spiritual direction of the nation. Then be available to Him—accepting whatever He calls you to do to shine His light to those around you.

Lord Jesus, I know You hear my prayers, and I praise You for being so near to those who seek You. Thank You for cleansing me of my sin through Your death and resurrection. Father, countless devastations are occurring in our nation and throughout the world, and these events are causing people to ask questions. They are frightened, in need, confused, and hurting. Their hearts are crying out for answers, Lord, but they are seeking solutions to their pain in places that only offer empty, temporary relief.

Father, please turn the spiritual tide of our nation—show the lost that the way, the truth, and the life can only be found in You. You have called believers to be Your ambassadors here on earth—You call us by Your own name! Yet we have not always represented You well. Father, help us humble ourselves, stir us to pray, make us hunger for Your presence, and show us the wickedness of our ways so that we may turn from them.

Father, please hear from heaven, forgive our sin, and heal our land! We know Your eyes are open to our troubles, and You are attentive to our cries. Thank You for answering us, turning this tide, and hearing our prayers. In Jesus' name, Amen. (See 2 Chronicles 7:12–15.)

WEEK 7: THE FINANCIAL CRISIS

Pray for God to turn the tide of our nation's current economic difficulties. The financial crisis that has overtaken the United States and countries around the world has been developing for a long time—and it appears to be more complicated and far more devastating than anyone could have imagined. Although some people are still doing relatively well, there are many who are suffering greatly.

Eventually, the difficulties of this crisis will touch every area of our society and will have repercussions for generations to come. As you go before the throne of grace this week, ask the Father to help those who are struggling financially—those who are out of work, those who are having a hard time making ends meet, who are losing their houses, and more. Also ask the Father to help people throughout our land understand that He is our Provider. Wealth and possessions are never a good foundation for a person's life because they can fade away. But when you and I build our lives on the truth of God's Word, we will not be shaken.

> **When you and I build our lives on the truth of God's Word, we will not be shaken.**

Lord God Almighty, we acknowledge You as our great Provider and Sustainer. This financial situation is overwhelming for us, but we know that You have all power to make wealth and to redeem us from our indebtedness. Deliver us from this crisis, Lord God. Comfort those in our nation who are hurting, and show them the unshakable foundation of Your Word. Reveal to us Your glory so that we will know You are God and that from Your hand comes every good thing—including temporary things like the food we eat daily and eternal provision such as the salvation of our souls. Surely, Father, the person who trusts in You will never lack any good thing. Thank You for hearing my prayer. In Jesus' name, Amen. (See Deuteronomy 8:18.)

WEEK 8: INCREASING TAXATION

Pray for God to stop the tide of increasing taxation in our nation so that faithful believers and churches can continue to fund missions throughout the world. It is astounding to realize that Christians in the United States fund 85 percent of the world's missions. It is no wonder, then, that when the enemy strikes out at believers in our country, he aims at the source of where they do so much good, which is their ability to give.

This week, please continue to pray for God to halt any attempts to increase our taxes so that faithful Christians and churches can continue to give, spreading the Good News of salvation to the ends of the earth—and that we as Christians will continue to give as generously as we can, even when our own finances are tight.

O God, You are testing our nation and purifying us as silver refined. Too often, we have trusted in our own resources, wealth, and possessions for our security; and we have, at times, failed to honor You by forgetting the hurting believers in other nations. Remind us of what is important, Father. Show us yet again that You alone are our security—the only One who truly provides for us. Protect us from the oppressive burden of further taxation so that we may continue our glad giving to the cause of the gospel.

Guard us from anyone who would attempt to rule us by controlling the crops we've harvested with our own hands. Set us free so that we can continue funding missions to every nation on earth. We thank You, Father, that whenever we have gone through fiery trials and floods of adversity in this nation, You've brought us back to a place of abundance. Please do so once again, O God! We praise You and thank You for hearing the prayers of Your people. In Jesus' name, Amen. (See Psalm 66:10–12.)

WEEK 9: INCREASING UNEMPLOYMENT

Pray for God's provision and protection for the unemployed and for wisdom on how the church can minister to them in their time of need. As we continue in prayer for our nation, we should remember our fellow Americans who have been hit so hard during these difficult financial times—especially those who have lost their jobs. We also need to ask God how we as the church can help our families, friends, and neighbors who are unemployed and need our assistance.

As James 2:15–16 asks, "If a brother or sister is without clothing and in need of daily food, and one of you says to them, 'Go in peace, be warmed and be filled,' and yet you do not give them what is necessary for their body, what use is that?"

Ask the Father to help us be proactive in showing His love to others.

We must ask the Father to help us be proactive in showing His love to others, encouraging them in their walks with Him, and leading them into growing relationships with Him.

> *Father God, my heart is heavy for those who have lost their jobs and are experiencing such disheartening financial difficulties. Lord, please comfort them, give them hope, and provide for them in a way that encourages them with the knowledge of Your love for them.*
>
> *Father, if there is a way You would have me or my church reach out to those in need in my community, please show me and empower me to be obedient to Your call. Give me the courage to be Your representative to the souls I know who are broken and discouraged. God, You have promised to supply all our needs according to Your riches in glory in Christ Jesus. Help me deliver this message of hope and the gospel of salvation to those who are in such desperate need. Thank You for hearing my prayer and the cries of Your people. In Jesus' name, Amen.* (See Philippians 4:19.)

WEEK 10: THE RAPID EROSION OF OUR LIBERTIES

Pray for God to deliver our nation from the rapid erosion of our liberties. When we originally prayed during the 140 Days of Prayer for the nation, the halfway point fell on September 11, 2010. Our minds were set on what had happened just nine years before during the worst terroristic attack on U.S. soil.

As believers, we should be aware of how people despise the liberties we have as Americans—the freedoms of religion, speech, and self-determination that are enumerated in our Constitution and Bill of Rights. It is a crucial reminder that there are individuals both here and abroad who are actively working to erode our liberties so they can take control of this nation. We must pray for God's protection against them and any schemes they may conspire to commit.

Lord God, You teach us that Christ has freed us from the power of sin and the grave through the cross. It was because of this liberty that the Founding Fathers of our nation were able to declare with confidence that You, our wonderful Creator, had endowed us with certain inalienable rights. Help us therefore, Father, to keep standing firm. Protect us from any who would erode our freedoms and try to subject us to a yoke of slavery.

Lord, we may not understand their schemes and tactics, but You promised that if we would put our hope in You, You would keep us safe from their snares. Thank You for being our shield and our salvation. I praise Your holy name and give You thanks for hearing my prayer. In Jesus' name, Amen. (See Galatians 5:1.)

WEEK 11: CONFUSION AND CORRUPTION

Pray for God to deliver us from the corruption and confusion that infects our government. Almost every day, we are confronted with more evidence of corruption in our government on both sides of the aisle. Consider the absolutely dangerous and destructive precedent this sets. When some of those who make and enforce the laws see themselves as above them, to the nation they set the terrible example of *do as we say, not as we do.*

Yet the Bible is clear, "He who digs a pit will fall into it" (Proverbs 26:27). Those who legislate regulations for their own advancement or to control the people will be thwarted by the very rules they create. As God's people, we must pray that the Lord will convict those who abuse the political process so that they will turn to Him and represent the people with truthfulness and dignity.

Father, thank You for loving and protecting Your people. We pray for those who serve as leaders in our government—that they would seek You and submit themselves to You. We know that there are those who would lead us away from Your best for our land. Father, You know them by name and love them. Shed light on any who would lead us astray so that they realize their sinfulness and repent of their wrong choices. We ask that You would draw them to Yourself, convict them of their sins, and bring them to salvation.

Contend with their plans, Lord—do not allow those who seek to confuse or control the people to prosper. Thank You for being our righteous Judge and King. We praise You for hearing our prayers and bringing hidden things to light. In Jesus' name, Amen. (See Isaiah 3:12–13.)

WEEK 12: THE WAR AGAINST JESUS

Pray for God to reveal Himself to those who oppose Jesus, and ask Him to save them in a powerful way. For those of us who believe, there is no more beautiful name in heaven or on earth than Jesus. But for those who do not understand what Christ accomplished on the cross, His name is confusing and even offensive. They do not realize who He is or the love and forgiveness He offers to us. Rather, Satan has convinced them of the lie that Jesus wants to remove their freedom. Therefore, many unbelievers battle against Him—fighting to take prayer and Bible study out of schools, spurning any mention of Him in public life, and trying to silence those who preach the gospel.

As those who have received His awe-some salvation, we must pray that God will reveal Himself powerfully to those who do not know Him. Ask the Father to show them that the One whom they war against is the One who could show them true liberty—healing all the wounds and answering all the questions they hold in their hearts.

> **Ask the Father to show them that the One whom they war against is the One who could show them true liberty.**

> *Jesus, thank You for being our Lord and Savior—for dying on the cross to give us freedom from sin and death. We love You and devote ourselves to You and to the proclamation of the gospel. Father, we pray for those who do not know You—especially those who fear You so greatly that they consider You and Your people their enemies. Help us to tell them the truth of salvation, regardless of whether they persecute us or accuse us wrongly. We know that we already belong to the kingdom of heaven and that they will perish if they do not accept the truth. Help us to stand strong for the sake of Your name and be as loving and forgiving as You would be.*
>
> *Help us to follow in Your footsteps, as the disciples and prophets did before us. Prepare our hearts for repentance, Lord, and give us Your words so that many can be brought to Your salvation. Thank You for hearing our prayers. We praise You that this is not an occasion for fear but an opportunity to bring in a plentiful harvest of souls. In Jesus' name, Amen.* (See Matthew 5:10–12.)

WEEK 13: TERRORISM

Pray for God's protection against terrorism and ask that Muslims throughout the world will come to know Jesus as their Savior. One of the greatest threats confronting us as a nation is that of terrorist attacks. Unlike the overt aggression we may experience from another country—which we can deal with diplomatically and militarily—the threat of terrorism is much more difficult to predict and prevent.

Thankfully, we know nothing is impossible for God. Ask the Lord to protect the nation from groups that send out terrorists and from those cells that are already planted within the United States, intent on doing harm. Also, ask the Father to save the men and women who are so filled with hate and so desperately without hope that they would participate in these destructive homicide bombings. They need the peace and purpose that can only be found through the Lord Jesus.

Father, thank You for safeguarding Your people and for giving us refuge under Your wings of protection. Truly, Your faithfulness is a shield and bulwark for us. Therefore, we will not be afraid of the terror by night or of the arrow that flies by day—of pestilence, darkness, or destruction.

Lord, even if those who wish to do us harm are able to attack, we will not be afraid. We know that in You is eternal life, and no one can take that from us. Ultimately, no one can snatch us out of Your hand or thwart Your plans.

Still, Father God, our hearts are broken for the Muslims throughout the world who have been taught to hate You and Your people from birth. Lord, show them the truth; reveal Your salvation to them in a powerful way. Give them hope and purpose. Remove the bitterness and fill them with Your love. God Most High, You are our dwelling place. We praise You for hearing our prayers and for being our unfailing tower of strength and safety. In Jesus' name, Amen. (See Psalm 91:4–9.)

WEEK 14: TURNING AWAY FROM ISRAEL

Pray for God to protect Israel, for the United States to continue to be her most faithful ally, for Jews worldwide to be saved, and for even her enemies to receive salvation through Jesus Christ. Throughout history, God has always had a very special relationship with the people of Israel. He established the nation saying, "The LORD your God has chosen you to be a people for His own possession out of all the peoples who are on the face of the earth. The LORD did not set His love on you nor choose you because you were more in number than any of the peoples, for you were the fewest of all peoples, but because the LORD loved you and kept the oath which He swore to your forefathers" (Deuteronomy 7:6–8).

The Father is still active in keeping His covenant with His people— drawing Jews throughout the world back to Himself and showing them

Pray that the United States will recognize the importance of Israel and support her.

that Jesus is the promised Messiah. Please pray that, as a nation, the United States will recognize the importance of Israel and support her. Also, pray that Jews worldwide will accept Him as their Savior and that even Israel's enemies will accept the gospel of salvation.

God of Abraham, Isaac, and Jacob, Lord of the Living Word, You keep Your covenant to a thousand generations. Thank You for being so faithful to Israel and for keeping Your promise to reestablish her in the land of her inheritance. Father, we pray that our country would take Your covenant with Israel seriously— understanding that you bless those that support her and curse those who oppose her.

We know that from her came our Savior—the Lord Jesus Christ. And in Him, all the people of the earth have been offered the gift of salvation. May the people of Israel acknowledge their guilt, seek

Your face, and accept Your Son—the Messiah. Truly, Jerusalem has become a cup of trembling for all the nations, so we pray that even her enemies would know You as Lord and Savior and through You have everlasting peace. We praise You for hearing our prayers and for keeping all Your promises. In Jesus' name, Amen. (See Genesis 12:3.)

WEEK 15: REAFFIRMING OUR NATION'S CHRISTIAN HERITAGE

Pray for our leaders to reaffirm our Christian heritage, and pray for biblical principles to return to the forefront of American life and law. There is absolutely no better way for a nation to function than with the Word of God as its guide and standard. We saw in chapter 10 that as Joshua was about to lead Israel into the Promised Land, the Lord told him, "This book of the law shall not depart from your mouth, but you shall meditate on it day and night, so that you may be careful to do according to all that is written in it; for then you will make your way prosperous, and then you will have success" (Joshua 1:8).

Pray that our leaders will go back to the basics—affirming our Christian heritage and seeking biblical principles by which to govern our nation.

America's Founding Fathers understood this, so they based the Constitution and the laws of our country on the principles they found in Scripture. As Christians, we understand that the reason this great experiment in democracy has been such an astounding success is because it was established on God's Word. Therefore, let us pray that our leaders will go back to the basics—affirming our Christian heritage and seeking biblical principles by which to govern our nation.

Father, You have taught us that the nations and peoples who claim You as Lord will be blessed and will prosper. We thank You for showing this to be true, and we thank You for Your great blessings on this country. Yet Father, we know that the people of our land have turned away from Your Word—seeking the wisdom of man over the principles found in Scripture.

Lord, please forgive us. Turn our hearts back to You in confession and repentance. Show our leaders there is truly no better way to govern than by obedience to You and Your commands. Help them to reaffirm our Christian heritage and reestablish Your biblical precepts as the basis of American society and law. Thank You for hearing our prayers, Father. Please continue to lead and bless this land. In Jesus' name, Amen. (See Psalm 33:12.)

WEEK 16: THE UNBORN

Pray that the practice of killing the unborn will end and that all affected by it will find forgiveness and redemption through Jesus Christ. Life is a wonderful gift that has been given to us by God. Sadly, when we do not value life as we should or acknowledge it as coming from Him, we experience consequences that devastate us individually and as a nation.

This week please pray that our country will once again acknowledge and respect the sanctity of life. Please also intercede for those who are experiencing the consequences of viewing people—whether unborn, young, old, or disabled—as being expendable. Pray that they will find redemption through Jesus Christ—the One who loves them and gives eternal life to all who seek Him.

Father, from the moment of conception, You form our inward parts—You weave each of us together within our mothers' wombs. Thank You, Lord, for making us in such a wonderful and awe-inspiring way—every one of us so detailed and complex—with gifts, talents, and abilities unique to each individual. Our frames have never been hidden from You, though they may be concealed from the outside world or they appear to be failing us as we grow older. Your eyes see us—even when no one else does—and in Your book are written the days ordained for us.

Lord, we pray that You will change our nation—that we would again acknowledge that life is from You and that every person is precious in Your sight. Please help those who have forgotten this to experience Your forgiveness and redemption. And please defend the helpless souls who cannot protect themselves. Thank You for hearing our prayers, Father. In Jesus' name, Amen. (See Psalm 139:13–16.)

WEEK 17: THE BIBLICAL VIEW OF MARRIAGE

Pray for a return to a biblical view of marriage and the strengthening of the family throughout our nation. God created people to function best when they are in healthy relationships. In fact, after forming Adam, He proclaimed, "It is not good for the man to be alone" (Genesis 2:18), and He created Eve, thereby setting into motion His plan for the family.

Unfortunately, as our society rejects the Lord's purposes and design for marriage, individuals find themselves increasingly isolated and lonely. Please pray that our nation will return to a biblical understanding of marriage, and that the heavenly Father will strengthen families throughout our land.

God, we acknowledge that You formed us for healthy, meaningful relationships—with Yourself, family, and people we encounter at church, the workplace, school, and elsewhere. Yet the more we violate Your principles in our interactions, the more isolated and fractured a society we become.

Father, please restore us; return us to a right view of Your standards for the family and to godly communion with one another. We need Your help to love others unconditionally, as You love us. Make us an example of Your grace. Use Your people to show the world what fulfilling families and relationships look like so that the lost will come to know You and be saved. Thank You for transforming this country and for hearing our prayers. In Jesus' name. Amen. (See Genesis 2:24.)

WEEK 18: NATURAL DISASTERS

Please pray for protection from natural disasters and for believers and churches to take every opportunity to minister to those who experience them. Earthquakes, tsunamis, tornadoes, floods, droughts, wildfires, and other natural phenomena can occur without warning and completely devastate the areas they strike. Many disagree as to how they arise, why they have increased in recent years, and whether or not God allows them for a purpose. However, one thing is for sure—they remind us how fleeting and uncertain life truly is.

Therefore, as we pray for protection from natural disasters this week, let us also ask the Lord for wisdom to answer people's questions about them when they do occur. Pray that believers will comfort the hurting, minister to their needs, and tell them about the life that can never be taken away: eternal life found in Jesus Christ.

> Pray that believers will . . . tell them about the life that can never be taken away: eternal life found in Jesus Christ.

Lord God, we pray for protection from the increasing natural disasters that are taking place in our world. Our hearts are heavy over the immense loss of life that has occurred over the last few years due to them, and we pray for comfort for those who have been affected—that they may know You as Lord and Savior. We ask for wisdom to address the questions people have about You. Please help us to minister to them in meaningful ways, telling them about Your kingdom, which cannot be destroyed or shaken.

Show us how to serve You most effectively during times of tragedy and distress, not worrying about our own losses, but demonstrating Your grace and goodness to others with love, reverence, and awe. We praise You because we know You can work through anything to reveal Yourself to those who are lost. Thank You for hearing our prayers and for healing those who are hurting. In Jesus' name, Amen. (See Hebrews 12:25–29.)

WEEK 19: WORLDWIDE REVIVAL

Please pray for our nation to be an example of Christian values to other countries, and pray for spiritual awakening and revival around the world. Although the United States of America can be a model of liberty to other countries, we have the greatest impact when we exemplify our Christian values. We see this vividly illustrated in the Old Testament. When Israel followed God faithfully, people from other lands acknowledged Him as Lord as well.

Pray that the Father will change the hearts and minds of our citizens, in the hope that through our example, people from every nation, tribe, and tongue will praise His name.

Therefore, let us pray that the Father will change the hearts and minds of our citizens, in the hope that through our example, people from every nation, tribe, and tongue will praise His name.

Father, how our hearts long to see every nation throughout the earth praise Your holy and wonderful name. The loving-kindness You have shown us is beyond measure, and we desire for people everywhere to know Your eternal provision of salvation through Jesus Christ. So, Lord, please make the United States of America a light to the nations and an example of the Savior's love and grace. May people not only know political freedom because of our country, but may they also come to understand the spiritual freedom from sin that You have so graciously provided for us. Thank You for hearing our prayers and bringing revival to people all over the world. In Jesus' name. Amen. (See Psalm 117.)

WEEK 20: PRAISE TO GOD FOR WHAT HE WILL ACCOMPLISH

Praise God for all He is doing to heal our land. Thank you so much for devoting yourself to prayer for the United States. We know that when God's people come together, He is faithful to answer and move in unimaginable ways. This week, spend time praising Him for all He's doing in our nation. We look forward to seeing how He will change the lives of families, communities, and our country in the coming days.

Lord God Almighty, we give praise for all You are doing and will do in our nation. Thank You for reviving the church in our land and for bringing spiritual awakening to unbelievers. We're grateful for the ways You're transforming our lives, restoring this great country, and making Yourself known to our fellow Americans.

Lord, we may never know of all Your works, and that is all right. But we glory in the knowledge that You alone are God—the Holy One who hears the prayers of His people and beautifies the afflicted with salvation. To You be all honor, glory, and worship now and forevermore—in America and all over the world. In Jesus' name, we pray. Amen. (See Psalm 149.)

HOW *YOU* CAN HELP TURN THE TIDE

1. *"As you begin to pray for our nation, it is important that you prepare your own heart first—going before the Father and making sure you have no unfinished business with Him."*

What do you need to do to prepare your heart before coming before the Father on behalf of others? Spend some time in honest prayer with God, asking Him to reveal the places in your heart and life that need to change. Ask God to forgive you for the sin He points out and to help you make the needed changes in your life.

2. *"Ask the Lord to change the spiritual direction of the nation. Then be available to Him—accepting whatever He calls you to do to shine His light to those around you."*

What might God be calling you to do in order to shine His light to others? Are you ready and willing to accept His call? By responding to His leading, you will do your part in helping to turn the tide of our country.

3. *"When we do not value life as we should or acknowledge it as coming from Him we experience consequences that devastate us individually and as a nation."*

What consequences do you think Dr. Stanley is referring to in the statement above? In addition to the more obvious ways of valuing life (of the unborn, the elderly, the disabled), what other ways can you personally value the lives of others? Each instance of love shared is one more effort to turn the tide away from destruction and toward our nation's rescue.

CHAPTER 14

BELIEVE!

Refuse to Give In or Give Up

I've seen our nation go through many times of crisis, from both foreign and domestic causes. One of the most powerfully impressionable times for me, however, was at the onset of the United States' involvement in World War II.

I was nine years old when Japanese aircraft bombed the naval base at Pearl Harbor on that otherwise quiet Sunday, December 7, 1941. By Monday, December 8, the United States had declared war on the assailing Japanese forces.

At the time, Universal-International news reporter Fred Maness declared, "The attack on Pearl Harbor united Americans as never before in history. In the explosions at Pearl Harbor there was forged the will for complete and absolute victory over the forces of evil."

I saw it with my own eyes. Americans responded in a way I will never forget. Young men from sixteen years of age and older joined our nation's armed forces to fight for our freedom. Many of my friends' parents lined up to serve—intent on defending our country. They accepted the hardships of war with courage and tenacity. They refused to back down or surrender because what was at stake was far too important.

As a child, I had an overwhelming sense that Americans were not afraid of the challenges they faced. I understood that my fellow citizens were bravely determined to safeguard the land they loved. We need that kind of courage and tenacity today.

I think we can all agree that a terrible tide is rising and our country is under serious threat. With the continuing onslaught of economic difficulties, socialism, increasing immorality, eroding personal freedoms, and lawmakers who often offer empty optimism rather than real solutions, we are facing a wave of trouble that promises to devastate our nation. If we don't act decisively and quickly, we will suffer loss and persecution unlike anything you and I have experienced before.

Now more than ever, we need the spirit of determination and the will for absolute victory over the forces that are assailing us—just as our fellow countrymen showed after the attack on Pearl Harbor.

I have been in ministry for more than fifty years, and I readily admit that I *could* become discouraged when I see the direction our country is taking—especially after all the sermons that have been preached on these very subjects. But I'm not giving in to pessimistic feelings, because I wholeheartedly believe that our good and all-powerful God understands our situation. I also have faith that His purposes continue to advance in our nation.

In fact, our foremost reason to believe that our future will be better is because *the Lord God Almighty is greater than any force on this earth.* The psalmist said it well:

> *Those who go down to the sea in ships,*
> *Who do business on great waters;*
> *They have seen the works of the LORD,*
> *And His wonders in the deep.*
> *For He spoke and raised up a stormy wind,*
> *Which lifted up the waves of the sea.*
> *They rose up to the heavens, they went down to the depths;*
> *Their soul melted away in their misery.*

They reeled and staggered like a drunken man,
And were at their wits' end.
Then they cried to the LORD in their trouble,
And He brought them out of their distresses.
He caused the storm to be still,
So that the waves of the sea were hushed.
Then they were glad because they were quiet,
So He guided them to their desired haven.
Let them give thanks to the LORD for His lovingkindness,
And for His wonders to the sons of men!
Let them extol Him also in the congregation of the people,
And praise Him at the seat of the elders. (Psalm 107:23–32)

The Father may have allowed us to face these difficulties in order to warn us of the deeper spiritual issues we face. However, when we turn back to Him and acknowledge Him as our Lord God, He will stem the tide and lead us to our desired haven.

> When we turn back to Him and acknowledge Him as our Lord God, He will stem the tide and lead us to our desired haven.

Therefore we must never give in to despair. He promises to respond to those who seek Him in humility and to look with favor on those who honor Him. So let us do so; let us humble ourselves before the Father and serve Him faithfully, knowing for certain He will forgive us and shower His favor upon us once again.

You see, God *will* bring genuine revival and spiritual awakening to our nation; however, we must wholeheartedly trust He will do so. Because according to Scripture, to *believe* He will help us indicates *we have faith in His leadership.* We must have confidence that He has the power, wisdom, resources, ability, insight, and love to change our lives and country. We should also be assured that no matter what He calls us to do, He is leading us in the very best path possible.

Do you believe these things? Do you have faith that the Lord can and will change this nation? And are you convinced that He is worthy of your absolute obedience, His commands are trustworthy, and His wonderful plans for your life are above and beyond all you could ask or imagine (see Ephesians 3:20)? You should be convinced, because it's all true.

The reality is our time is short. You and I do not know how much longer we have to influence those around us and affect the course of the country.

Thankfully, we still live in a nation where

- a person can walk down a street and pass out gospel tracts or Bibles to any person who will accept one.

- people can gather to sing praise songs and tell others the good news of salvation through Jesus Christ.

- churches can hold God-honoring worship services at any hour—whatever day of the week and as often as they please.

- ministries are free to publish Christ-centered resources in print and on the Internet and are able to broadcast the importance of a growing relationship with Jesus Christ on both radio and television.

Therefore, as believers, let us accept the challenges that are ahead with courage and tenacity.

> **Let us *believe* that the Lord will not only guide us through these troublesome times of rising tides, but will also use them to lead us to even greater purity and blessing.**

Let us make the most of these liberties and opportunities while we still have them. Let us influence those around us—our families, friends, co-workers, and church members—with the truth of God's Word. And let us *believe* that the Lord will not only guide us through these troublesome times of rising tides but will also use them to lead us to even greater purity and blessing.

Will we face setbacks as we try to reestablish strong Christian values and morality in our land? Yes we will. But is the Father still at work despite how things look? Absolutely!

We may not have experienced a definitive breakthrough yet, but every believer who commits himself or herself to obeying the Lord, reading His Word, praying, and speaking out boldly brings us one step closer every day.

So take part in being the real change this nation desperately needs. Allow the Father to work through you to turn this tide. Do not back down. Never surrender. What is at stake is far too important for us to ever give up.

Godly citizenship *can* make a difference. All that is necessary is that you believe.

Lord God Almighty—Maker of heaven, earth, and this nation—
teach us to truly believe and help our unbelief.
When disappointments come, strengthen our faith
and gird our hearts with Your unfailing love.
Give us the courage to walk in Your ways
to the glory of Your name.
We love this country,
and we desire for You to be exalted in it.
May our fellow Americans seek You for salvation
and follow Your commands with joy.
Father, guide our steps, give us Your words for Your people,
and allow Your light to shine through us
because we love and worship You.
Help us to endure so that we—and this nation—
may experience Your very best. Amen.

HOW *YOU* CAN HELP TURN THE TIDE

1. Dr. Stanley maintains, *"I'm not giving in to pessimistic feelings."*

In such troubled times, how can Dr. Stanley—and how can you—have the confidence not to give in to pessimistic feelings? How does maintaining our confident hope in Christ's provision and power help to turn back the tide? What can you do to bring your own feelings in line with this teaching?

2. *"Our foremost reason to believe that our future will be better is because* the Lord God Almighty is greater than any force on this earth."

Do you feel strongly in your faith that God is greater than the forces that upset your own personal life? Or do you feel overwhelmed and discouraged? What practical steps can you take to grow in your faith? Consider joining together with other people of faith; pray and study God's Word together. With this kind of fellowship, your faith will increase and you will be better equipped to serve your country.

3. *"We should be assured that no matter what He calls us to do, He is leading us in the very best path possible."*

Where does the kind of assurance that Dr. Stanley refers to come from? What difficult paths have you had to walk down? What good things did you discover in your journey? How can you apply what you've learned to being an active, godly citizen of the United States for the betterment of our country?

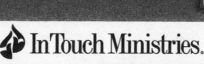

Pray.

Visit **intouch.org/prayerteam** and learn how you can intercede for our ministry by joining the Impact Prayer Team.

InTouch
Impact Team
Prayer Partnership